"Dream
and the way
will be clear,
Pray and the Angels
will hear,
Leap and the net
will appear."

Steve Seskin

The Cranky Guru - Adventures in Metaphysics

THE CRANKY GURU

Adventures in Metaphysics

PAUL L BENNETT

Title: The Cranky Guru - Adventures in Metaphysics
First published: 2014 by Paul L Bennett
Copyright: © 2014 Paul L Bennett
Editor: Cecily-Anna Bradley
Cover Design: Paul L Bennett
Printed by: InHousePublishing.com.au

National Library of Australia Cataloguing-in-Publications entry

Author:	Bennett, Paul (Author)
Title:	The Cranky Guru - Adventures in Metaphysics / Paul Bennett
ISBN:	9780992551902 (Paperback)
Subject:	Conduct of life
	Self-actualisation (Psychology)
	Self-consciousness (Awareness)
Dewey Number:	158.1

Contents

Foreword:
Professor David L Bennett AO

There is nothing ordinary about Paul Bennett—spiritualist, artist, inventor, teacher, musician, joke-teller, husband, father, mentor and friend. He is also The Cranky Guru and my very special, one and only brother. We grew up enjoying each other's company, amiably connected through music (he on violin, me on piano), rough-housing and rambling in the neighbourhood (the latter being an acceptable activity for children in the sixties) and sharing love and respect for our Mum (the tough one) and Dad (a commercial artist and self-taught jazz pianist with talent to burn). Although we've taken different life paths, we share a curiosity about existential matters, especially the mysteries of life, loving and living. Our conversations are never ordinary!

The Cranky Guru – Adventures in Metaphysics is a highly personal, self-effacing and often entertaining account of a spiritual journey. Its messages and stories reflect the benevolent and altruistic goals of the author, a man thoroughly versed in the writings of sages and philosophers from time immemorial. Paul simply wants the world to be a kinder and more compassionate place. He wants us to be more enquiring, more confident, and more prepared to believe that things will work out well (at least better) if we gently embrace a facilitating mindset. He believes in the intrinsic decentness of human beings and is keen to interact warmly with as many people as possible. He does this primarily through his Facebook page (facebook.com/paul.bennett.58118) and is both heartened and at times amused by the responses he receives to his invariably thought-provoking posts.

Much solid evidence sits behind many of the ideas and suggestions that *The Cranky Guru* brings to our attention here. Hopefulness, cheerfulness, mindfulness and kindness, for example, are attributes that bring favourable outcomes to many, comfort and encouragement to all. This inaugural book is a gem – not only will you enjoy reading it, it might just change your life.

Clinical Professor David Bennett AO, adolescent health physician at The Children's Hospital at Westmead.

Foreword:
Rabbi Zalman Kastel

I have known Paul for ten years. His white curls, bold dress sense, beaming face and happy spirit always make me smile.

This book you hold in your hands glows with positive energy, love and light. Its value increased by the fact that it has been written by someone well aware of the ugly, bad and sad.

Paul is the kind of man who strives to accept 'all that is'. However, like all of us, he is also susceptible to emotions that aren't synonymous with love and light. The story I would like to share with you is an example of a time Paul was less Happy Guru, more Cranky Guru.

Five years ago, Paul approached me about offering his services to assist the inclusive multi-faith-based diversity education organisation I lead, called Together for Humanity. He loved the concept – or so he thought – until I sent him an email that made him question his very involvement.

You see, Paul (a graphic designer by trade) had designed a new logo for our organisation. Its colours were bright, and featured two eyes, and neat shapes representing people from different faiths engaging with each other. The logo was circulated to the board of the Together For Humanity Foundation, which includes representatives of the Islamic, Christian and Jewish faiths—most of whom were happy with it. However, a Muslim member of our team objected to the eyes in the image. It represented a 'graven image' according to his understanding of his faith. As such, he did not feel represented by the logo.

I flicked an email to Paul about removing the eyes, and thought nothing of it.

Now, anger serves a purpose. It can alert us that something we deem precious has been violated, and in this case, Paul felt his artistic integrity was at stake. His belief was that eliminating the eyes was giving in to fundamentalism and threatening to stifle the creative potential of future Muslim Michaelangelos.

This was not a trivial matter to Paul or me and I respected the artistic principles he was prepared to fight for. So, over green tea, in a little café, I suggested there was another way to look at this conflict of values. The more useful question was, how do we build a tent that accommodates people with divergent views?

Paul sipped his tea—and though his mug still appeared more half-empty than full, he said he would have another go. A few days later—and after some meditation, Paul could see a compromise. He returned with a logo that was inclusive of all faiths, proving that while we're all prone to anger, indignation and everything in between, the secret of success is a little optimism and generosity of spirit—something Paul has in vast quantities, as I'm sure you're about to discover.

Rabbi Zalman Kastel, Together for Humanity Foundation
togetherforhumanity.org.au

Together for humanity

Introduction:
Why am I writing this book?

I seem to be taking two steps forward, one step back, two steps forward, one step back. Hey—that's two steps forward! I'm winning! Hooray!

Why am I writing this book? You probably won't know the answer, so I'll tell you. 'Now' is the right time. In fact, it's the *only* time to do anything, since I've never heard of anyone doing anything in the past or future. As a man in my 60s, I've had ample opportunity to experience life as an active participant, and more recently as a fascinated observer of the influences, the failures and the amazing successes of life. These are the things that make the story of who we are, life-defining and memorable. Many of us spend our lives yearning for things to make us 'more'. We feel that if we keep adding 'stuff'—newer car, better job, bigger house—then life will be better. But will it really ?

We miss so much in our incessant search for 'the next big thing', but what are we seeking? The missing intangible ingredient of course. That 'something' which will complete us. We don't really know what this 'something' is, we just know it's missing—and so the search begins. Everyone wants their life to be meaningful, and given the mind's tendency to judge (often harshly), we may think we're not measuring up compared to others. And yet, there isn't a sentient being on the planet who is *not* making a worthy contribution, even if the role they've chosen is to challenge others. Looking back on my life, I can plainly see how the adversity I've experienced has strengthened my character and created mental and spiritual growth.

The truth? We're all born loving, compassionate, and curious about the world in which we find ourselves. We instinctively 'know' we are good, that we belong and that we possess a strong desire to add value to our quality of life. However, we are also taught that Man is a greedy predator and intrinsically 'sinful' and that human nature is not to be trusted. So governments make laws with harsh punishments for wrongdoing which far outweigh any rewards for 'right-doing'. No wonder then, the beliefs of our societies become our individual beliefs as well, making us hesitant to act on our natural impulses. And what if there were no laws? Might we then learn to trust ourselves again? I want my book to tell this story. A story based on love, trust, understanding and acceptance. Whether we realise it or not, our spiritual awakening is inevitable. Although we may sometimes feel alienated, we have an instinctive sense of justice and a deep desire to help others. And even though we may sometimes be seen as distracted, naive and profoundly idealistic, we are here to provide a bridge between the visible and the invisible, to embrace our true potential and give hope to others. So, it is time now to accept who we really are.

Let the journey begin!

Chapter 1: 'Act as if'.

How I used metaphysics to renew my passport in three hours.

*"Dream and the way will be clear. . . Pray and the angels will hear. . .
Leap and the net will appear." — Steve Seskin*

"Darling, find the passports," said Tutti, my wife. I ran
upstairs to where the passports had rested unused
for the past few years. Mine? Check. Tutti's? Check.
My daughter Sonia's? Check. Bali, here we come!
I casually checked the expiry dates. Tutti... 2012. Sonia... 2013.
Paul... December 14th, 2011. I stood aghast. My passport had
expired that very day, and at 3pm tomorrow, we were leaving
for Denpasar! Now, you may find this strange, but I didn't panic.
I simply accepted "what is". Besides, I knew Tutti would do
enough panicking for both of us. I came downstairs to share my
bad news and sure enough, I got the predictable and justifiable
response. After all, we had been planning our trip for months,
so who's a silly man then? I am! Still, I felt no sense of dread,
stress or disappointment, just a total acceptance of the situation
as it was. Many years of meditation had completely changed my
outlook on life. In fact, Tutti's greatest concern is that I don't

worry about anything. I've learnt that all we really have to work with is what Eckhart Tolle coined 'The Power of Now' and this moment required some powerful work! The past is history, the future is a mystery and the moment is a gift. Our future was about to be created, its existence entirely dependent on what we believed. So, back to *my* moment. I sat down at my computer and googled 'Australian Passport Office' and 'fast-track passport renewal', only to discover there was a two-day turnaround time'. Wait a minute! Two days? Our plane was leaving at 3pm the following afternoon and we needed to check in at least one hour before. I calmly checked the facts. Passport office, open at 9am. Our pick up for the drive to the airport, 1pm. Arrive at airport 1.30pm—wait a minute! That only gives me THREE HOURS to change providence and travel to Bali with my family. But the official Australian Passport website said 'FAST TRACK: 2 DAYS!' Sounds impossible, yes? Maybe not...

Rule Number 1: It's not over till the plane takes off!

How is it that some people push on regardless against apparently insurmountable odds, while others simply throw in the towel and give up? Is it tenacity, pig-headedness, blind faith, crazy positive thinking? Or is it a deeper knowing, a heightened awareness, or an understanding of how to make things happen in our favour? Some might believe 'giving up' and 'acceptance' are the same thing, but they are actually very different. I'm going to share this fundamental difference with you, but before I do, let me clarify my point. 'Mindless positivity' in and of itself can sometimes work, but it's fraught with danger. I've attempted the 'you can do anything' approach based on various authors I've read and crashed so heavily that I barely survived to lick my financial wounds! No, there is a much deeper approach. One that aligns with and harnesses the energy of Universal Law. Let's call it 'engaging benevolence'.

Benevolence (*Noun*)

1) *The desire to do good by others; goodwill; charitableness; to be filled with benevolence towards one's fellow creatures.*

2) *An act of kindness; serving a charitable rather than a profit-making purpose: eg. a benevolent fund.*

Here's how I engaged benevolence to assist me in my present dilemma.

The Passport Office

I made sure I arrived at the passport office in good time (8:00am) and was happy to discover the office opened at 8:30am and not 9:00am. That's half an hour saved! As I waited, the reception filled to capacity with eager people from diverse cultural backgrounds all wanting to be first in line. When 8:30am finally arrived and the floodgates opened, there was a rush for the elevator. I could feel anxiety mingled with the natural discomfort associated with lift travel and the dead silence which seems mandatory in elevators as people strive to retain their personal space. Anyhow, as we rose to our floor, I asked loudly and happily, "Has everyone met?" There was immediate laughter which shattered the silence and the tense atmosphere. "You're all going to have a very successful morning," I said, "So don't worry about anything!" More laughter as we arrived at the 7th floor and a relaxed, much happier group piled out.

Many years earlier, I started a movement called the Lift Club (see Chapter 3) to promote 'friendship in tight spaces'. I had often observed the small miracle that takes place when the protective bubble around ones personal space is pricked and insular individuals momentarily become a group—and I'm convinced that humour contains healing and transformative energy for the greater good. But there was an even deeper purpose to my humour this particular morning, based on the esoteric premise, 'If you want something for yourself, give it to someone else'. The truth is, I was wanting *everyone* to be in a happy, receptive mood on this particular morning!

Remember, this particular little adventure is about providence. Beating the odds. So, as fate would have it, most of those entering the room turned left to Passport Applications, while I turned right to Passport Renewals and found myself first in line. As I approached the counter, I was confronted by the rock-hard visage of a woman in her late 60s, no doubt a 'career' government employee who had seen it all before. Even though I was aware she was not the passport official who would be interviewing me, I proceeded to tell her in a humorous fashion what a complete idiot I had been for not renewing my passport earlier, but that we were leaving for Bali tomorrow and could she please, *please* assist me? She had actually laughed at my "idiot" comment, and as she handed me my appointment number, I felt her entire demeanour soften to be replaced by a more compassionate energy. "Let's see what can be done," she said, as I sat and waited for my number to be called.

In every human interaction, we are dealing with an exchange of energy far more meaningful than is realised. As like energy attracts like, we have more chance of receiving a positive response from others, if we can project positive, benevolent energy into every exchange. As I sat waiting, I thought about how important it is to embrace and align with benevolent energy. You see, I was not just thinking what was best for me, but what represented the 'greater good' in this situation, and that was the creation of a happy holiday atmosphere for me and my family. This was the benevolent outcome I asked for. As I waited, I recited a benevolent prayer I had used in similar situations over many years:

"I ask for the most benevolent outcome to my present situation so I can travel to Bali with my family this afternoon at 3pm. I ask that this happen now in ways beyond my comprehension, but with the most benevolent outcome for all."

It's not possible to say the word 'benevolent' too many times. You may well drive your friends and family crazy (as I do), but it needs to become ingrained in your psyche because it is a word with enormous magical energy.

Finally, my number appeared on the screen and I headed for

the designated window. As I approached, I heard a harsh voice telling someone their papers were not complete and to go and fix them. The energy projected was of anger and frustration, and I hoped he was not going to be the one to handle my case. He wasn't, thankfully. The woman who had been the subject of his wrath picked up her papers and left hurriedly, as I approached the man who would be helping me with my conundrum. He was a rather rotund man with a good-natured, ruddy, freckled face and a wise, quizzical expression. "Hello," I said, and told him the story of how silly I had been and how I hoped he would be able to assist me.

I ruminated on the fact that if I had been one number earlier, I would have been confronted by Mr Harsh-and-Cranky instead of Mr Laid-Back-and-Friendly. Luck? Providence? Had my benevolent energy preceded me to the 'right' window? He took my papers and efficiently browsed the contents containing the details of my case and the passport photos I had taken of myself the night before (and spent hours photo-shopping—call it vanity) to save time. "Please wait a moment," he said and left the booth briefly. "I'm sorry, we can't accept these photos," he said when he returned. "You'll need to get some professionally produced." Oh my God, no! This will take even more time! And

I thought my picture looked great. (Well, I may have *slightly* overdone the retouching, but in my view, it still looked like me.) I was told where the nearest photo booth was and I immediately took off through the driving rain which had started to bucket down.

A bad omen? Hopefully not. I found the photo booth and sat in front of the camera, drenched and bedraggled—not the image I was hoping to project for the next ten years. Photos in hand, I immediately sprinted back to Mr Laid-Back-and-Friendly who had very kindly kept his window free for my return. (Amazing in itself). After attaching my new (much less attractive) photos to my documents, he wished me good luck and directed me to the cashier's window. Here I was afforded another opportunity to tell my story and hopefully manifest another benevolent response. I was greeted by a middle-aged woman who listened to my story, with compassion and understanding on her face.

In the background, a cashier who had just left her window and overheard my predicament, grumpily interjected with, "Well, that's not likely to happen is it?" My heart sank. The nice cashier told me not to worry, saying quietly, "She's always like that." Always? A minute earlier and she would have been *my* cashier! The nice cashier even asked her cranky co-worker to wait a moment for our transaction to be completed so she could run my papers over to collections. What an angel! At this, I left to rush home with just packing my suitcase and a successful outcome on my mind.

You see, even when things seem impossible, follow the golden rule of metaphysics. Simply 'ACT AS IF' and nine times out of ten, things will work out in your favour. I never doubted I would make that flight and constantly visualised myself on that plane with my happy (and relieved) family. Sure enough, two hours later we drove back to the passport office to find my new passport waiting for me in collections, and we were on our way to the airport together! I found out later my eldest daughter Cecily-Anna had secretly asked my wife Tutti, "Mummy, if Daddy pulls this off, will you follow his philosophies?" To which she said, "Yes I will!" But I'm definitely not holding my breath!

My passport photo   *Their passport photo!*

Chapter 2: Destiny.

Magnetism, attraction and meeting my soulmate Tutti.

In spite of all that has transpired over the past 38 years between Tutti and me—the breathtaking highs and the disappointing lows—there is no doubt in my mind that we were meant to be together. She is my greatest teacher and my soulmate.

As flight Q35 taxied down the runway preparing to take off for Denpasar airport, I thought about the events of the past twenty-four hours and reflected on my life so far. Sixty-six years old, married to Tutti for 37 years, father of two wonderful daughters, Cecily-Anna and Sonia. I had great friends and interesting work in the advertising agency Tutti and I own. I looked across at Tutti contentedly settling into her seat, and smiled to myself. In spite of the challenges we had faced together, there was a lot of love there. I started thinking about the very first time I ever set eyes on her.

It was 1974 and I had just returned to Australia after an amazing twelve months studying in London on a Rotary Scholarship, followed by two months travelling through Europe. 1974 was definitely a life-defining year for me. Growing up in 'sleepy'

Brisbane in the 1960s was much like Dame Edna Everage's Moonee Ponds. Yet in London, there were more beautiful women than I could ever have imagined, all happy to engage with me. It was definitely an eye opener! Anyhow, on my return to Brisbane, I lasted just long enough to fulfil my Rotary commitments and then it was full steam ahead to Sydney to try my luck in the big smoke. Brisbane seemed so provincial after such a crazy, exciting year in Europe, and I had certainly acquired an unrealistic attitude towards romantic conquests after so many adventures.

Nevertheless, I continued in this way until one night, my girlfriend (of that week)—let's call her Sarah—invited me to a big party one Saturday night. The moment I arrived at the party and stepped into the crowded living room, Tutti caught my eye. No, that's not nearly strong enough a description of the emotions I felt looking at her for the first time. I was transfixed! I was in love! It was a cosmic connection of such power, I was helpless to resist. Sarah faded into oblivion, never to be seen again, as I elbowed people out of the way to get to Tutti. As I found out later, Tutti was there with her live-in bodybuilder boyfriend, Peter, but undaunted, I walked straight up to her and said, "Hi! I must take you out sometime." She told me much later her immediate thought was, "Uh oh! Not another guy trying to get it on!" Little did I know I had just met my soul mate. That very week after our meeting, Tutti told her mother, "Mummy, if I ever marry anyone, I'm marrying this guy!" Is it possible to know? Is there such a thing as destiny? I do believe so. Here's how I think it works.

Destiny

You may need to suspend disbelief for a few moments and just hear me out as I espouse some esoteric ideas you may not have embraced before. Firstly, it's my belief that there is such a thing as reincarnation and being a JuBu, (Jewish Buddhist) of course I'd think that! Accepting there is such a thing and that we spend eternity living myriad lives, would it not also be feasible to assume that we'd be given some carte blanche as to what those lives might be?

When I consider my life and the lives of those around me, I wonder many things. Did I choose my parents and the environment in which I grew up and developed? Did I choose the artistic and musical talents I displayed from an early age? At eight years old, my brother Prof. David Bennett AO, proclaimed to anyone who would listen, "I'm going to be a doctor!" and I was equally sure I would live an artist's life. I believe there *is* precognition in these matters and then, as we land with a bump on Mother Earth, free will kicks in and that's when the fun really starts! All lines to the 'larger reality' get blurred and the journey of discovery and growth, the challenges, the adversity, the predetermined hurdles we'll encounter, make for an interesting ride. As John Lennon sang, "Life happens while you're making other plans".

Based on our most recent previous existence—and I'm not talking about karma here—since there can't be such a thing within the principles I'm espousing—we would choose our next life circumstance, the country of our birth, the details of our experiential existence (for example whether we're rich or poor, male or female and who our partners through life will be). As you can see, this list could go on and on to include ethnicity, gender, physical appearance, whether we're beautiful or ugly, ill or healthy. The possibilities are endless. In the eternal moment of now, where lives simultaneously converge, I chose Tutti and she chose me.

On that magical night, when our eyes met across that crowded room, the planets converged, there was thunder and lightning and a giant cosmic spark arced between us, overriding all previous arrangements and sealing the pact we had made with each other for eternity. Thirty-eight years later, we're still together and ever pondering the mysteries of our relationship. We have families of course, but we also have 'psychic families', those souls we are meant to interact with in this lifetime. Tutti was no coincidence.

This subject fascinated me so much, that I sought answers from an amazing channel, Andrea Seiver, PhD, (andreaseiver.com) who has over 30 years experience in the helping/healing professions. A practicing psychologist for 26 years, she became a channel in 1986 for Vywamus, a teacher from the higher levels of consciousness who has a special interest in humanity. Since 1988, Seiver has worked with Vywamus to offer channelled readings as well as courses in channelling and spiritual growth in Boston and in the US. (She has also recently completed channelling a book from Vywamus entitled, *The Next Big Bang: The Explosion of Human Consciousness.*)

I posted my 'destiny' question to Vywamus. His response to me, through Andrea, was extraordinary and corroborated my belief. Here is my letter and Vywamus' response:

My letter to Vywamus

Dear Vywamus,

My question relates to the issue of DESTINY. I've been married to my wife Tutti for 37 years now and we have two beautiful daughters, Cecily-Anna and Sonia. Although I had been a serial dater with many girlfriends prior to meeting Tutti, it seemed at the time that our meeting was 'destined' to take place. A 'Cosmic Connection' as it were. Can you please explain to me if 'soul mate connections' such as ours are predetermined and how they are established before the experiential existence? Truth, Love and Light,

Paul

Vywamus' response

Dear Paul,

This is indeed a question of interest to many of you on earth at this time. In a few words, yes, the soul mate bond is predetermined, but this is a predetermination that each of your souls helped design long before you came into bodies.

From before the beginning, you and every other human are— and always were—one with the Oneness of Being (the Prime or

Universal Field of Energy). This Energy is constantly creating itself into an infinite number of forms. Forms which are still always one with the universal Oneness, and never separate from it. Every one of these forms has awareness and will, and its own unique patterns of the Primal Energy, and every one of these forms is a matrix from which new forms can evolve. In the case of soul creation, for simplicity we can call these matrices "over souls." (Various writers have defined the term "over soul" in different ways, but this is how I use it here.)

Supported by guidance from the very highest levels of Energy, an over soul may choose to evolve in many possible ways. It may evolve into a single soul, a pair or group of individual souls, or even into a single soul divided into two or more parts. This evolution begins at very high levels, on the spiritual or numinous energy planes, and long before an individual soul's journey into the astral and physical realms of existence.

As souls from the same over soul make this journey toward the level of physical incarnation, because they have so many energy patterns in common, there is a feeling of kinship and familiarity among them, a feeling of being bonded and 'at home' with each other. This is what you know as the soul mate connection. Before taking on a body, you may make agreements with each other about what paths you will take, when you will meet, and so on. And because of your similar energy patterns, you are often drawn to similar times, places and activities in physical life. When you then encounter each other in bodily form, you often experience a sense of recognition at a very deep level—sometimes with great clarity. At other times you come to know each other more gradually, starting with a simple, growing feeling of belonging or being 'right' with each other. There is often a sense of 'of course!' about this soul bond you have. Then, because being together in physical life is so comforting and satisfying, and thus allows you to focus also on reaching your other goals in life, you meet often and become more and more familiar with each other on the physical level as you develop a physical history.

Of course, every soul has its individual paths of development as well, and you bring your unfinished learning and "baggage" into any physical life you enter. So meeting your soul mate in a particular life is not always a wonderful panacea for all the suffering and confusion you may have experienced in other lives.

Much of the joy and peace in living a physical life with a soul mate depends on how much you each have already evolved. If one or both of you still has many issues to deal with, then being together may be a great support for doing so, but you will still have many ups and downs, and much hard work to do. It will not be the fairy tale existence that you might hope for. On the other hand, when each of you has done a good measure of evolving, your life together—though it will of course still have some of the challenges of any physical existence—usually, at its core, be quite joyful, peaceful, and relatively uncomplicated. So if this is you, enjoy!

It is important to note, by the way, that for soul mates, or for anyone who is living such a happy and relatively struggle free life as I describe, one of the great gifts you can give to the world is to spread this joy and comfort to all who come in contact with you. You do this mainly just by being and radiating your energies out to others. You do not have to argue them out of their suffering, or get them to change their ways, or take on the responsibility for their awakening.

Simply by allowing yourself to enjoy the happiness you have, and meeting life's challenges with as much grace and balance as you can, you send them joyful energy and provide them with a model. Through you they see that such a life as yours is actually possible, and they receive hope and inspiration, if they are open to it. This may even lead them to a turning point they need, and make all the difference in their lives.

I hope you and Tutti, and others reading this who have reached some degree of balance and happiness in this life, will make the intention to continue to enjoy each other and your life to the fullest possible, and to consciously send out and share your blessings and your light with others around you. Your world needs that joy. Thank you for writing and for sharing your joy on this page.

Warmly,

Vywamus

You see, I believe we are blocked from full awareness for the duration of our journey, thereby affording us the exquisite joy of rediscovery. What a great game this Game of Life is! Like a play, we choose our role, the settings, props and fellow actors and then perform our parts to the best of our ability. Recently, I was sitting with my elderly mum in Greenwich hospital as she recovered from her hip operation and I told her about my thoughts on destiny. In response, she told me this story. "When I was 4 years old in the 1920s, my parents owned a small corner store in Brisbane. Every day after school, a little six-year-old boy would come and buy a toffee apple made by my mum. Twenty years later, I married him!" And the rest, as they say, is history.

My parents: Cecil George and Ray Bennett

Chapter 3: Friendship.
The Lift Club Project

Many believe we are born with the ability to express unconditional love,
but have learned from those around us that we cannot safely show it.
So how about 'unconditional friendship' as a possible starting point?

We've all ridden in elevators. It's obvious to me that they provide a great opportunity to meet people, but what has always astounded me, is how quickly people 'shut down' on entering, followed by navel gazing and floor-number counting. After all, it's not easy to be in our 'own' space in such a small area, so we might as well communicate for the duration of the short journey. That's the plan, at any rate.

I first introduced this concept several years ago. I launched a Lift Club website which gave anyone who wanted to live my philosophy that 'strangers are just friends waiting to happen' all the tools they'd need to break down social barriers. I had games they could play, ice breakers they could use and profound questions they could ask their fellow lift travellers—a variety of exercises designed to help people smile, relax and engage. My Lift Club generated so much interest that a reporter was assigned by *The Sydney Morning Herald* to write about it. One Monday morning, at 9am, we found ourselves standing at the base of Chifley Tower in the middle of Sydney CBD in peak hour. For those of you who don't know Chifley Tower, it's a very tall building and one of the city's corporate hubs, chock-full of solicitors, barristers and big business types of every kind.

For this experiment, I decided on an exercise I call the Pavarotti Game. I had prepared song sheets in advance with the words to *Put on a Happy Face* printed in big letters. As we piled into one of the many lifts at ground level (which was full to bursting), I greeted everyone warmly, as if they were expecting me and waiting for the meeting to start. Certainly some people looked shocked, but most were amused. As Lift Captain, I introduced myself and my club and proceeded to hand out song sheets.

I'm a professionally-trained opera singer, and as I started to sing and encourage others to join in, a fascinating variety of reactions ensued. A few stripe-suited gentlemen remained stoic, while others grasped this crazy opportunity with both hands and sang along lustily with me! As people reached their floors, I asked them what they thought of the experience. Many thanked me, and said it was the most fun they'd had in the building to date. Others, like the poker-faced barristers, couldn't leave fast enough without comment. Social activism at its best, I thought!

We travelled up and down the Chifley Tower lift about ten times on that busy Monday morning, with responses to the journeys being different every time. Regardless of what people thought of the experience, we managed to bring people together in ways they had never experienced before. As an experiment in human nature, it was truly fascinating. It brought into sharp relief the countless different attitudes and beliefs with which people create their lives.

When we think of the humble elevator, what do we think of? Yes, it's a method of transport between floors in tall buildings, but I think it can be so much more. All we have to do is explore its enormous potential to help people communicate better with each other; to create a 'Lift Philosophy' and strategy to negate the fear people appear to have of bonding in tight spaces.

Having always had a strong affinity with altruism, my dearest wish is that The Lift Club will help people feel better about themselves and then inspire them to pass the good vibes on to others. I hope it will create a snowball effect of good energy, and in a small way make the world a happier place.

Now, the sixty-four thousand dollar question is, why don't we talk to each other? In elevators, on buses and trains, the overwhelming lack of communication is the same. I truly believe that strangers are just friends waiting to happen which is why I started The Lift Club in the first place. The club creates opportunities for people to meet and become friends. As so many of us have discovered, the simple act of extending the hand of friendship can have far reaching benefits and for someone as gregarious as me, it was a situation that needed fixing. So what else could I do but become a social activist?

Why is a lift the perfect place to bond with people?

1) You have to be there anyway.

2) You're already out of your comfort zone.

3) Everyone else in the lift is in the same boat.

4) The journey is short, so you might as well MAKE IT FUN!

My objectives for starting The Lift Club were simple. Firstly, I love the idea of promoting friendly interaction—indeed, friendship— between strangers. After all, you never know the joy that can be experienced from letting new people into your life, until you do!

Secondly, I want to create good energy—which I call 'heart' energy—and inspire others to do the same. After all, I believe it's our duty as loving, sentient beings, to project the very best energy possible, straight from the heart.

Third? I want to create a club environment. It's a simple truth that once you engage people in conversation, in a lift, for example, a cosmic reaction takes place. The people you engage with become a group and you soon realise it doesn't matter that you don't all know each other. You'll have a lot of fun proving this for yourself!

Finally, as with anything in life, I think it's incredibly important to have fun, which is one of the main premises of The Lift Club. We live in a sombre, strife-filled world, so what better way to bring a bit of light into your life, than by turning the dull elevator ride into a ship of fun, amidst the turbulent seas of trouble in which we live? Every one of us can make a choice between being miserable and being happy, so we might as well be happy and share it with others.

Want to spread the friendship and joy of your own Lift Club? Anyone can do it, and I've devised a few simple exercises and strategies to help you on your way.

1) Engage people in the lift by telling them straight away you are a member of The Lift Club and that you have taken an oath to befriend all fellow travellers. A natural response to this may be to ask about the club (or shrink away into the corner while giving you strange looks. Just remember, you win some, you lose some!) Introduce yourself, and the friendship process has begun!

2) Use mind games to break the ice. See below for a few examples I've used myself, to great effect.

MIND GAMES

Create your Lift Club
Ask everyone in the lift their names, then introduce them to each other. If there is only one other in the lift, introduce yourself first, then ask them their name. This is your job as Lift Captain. You'll need to be quick though—lift meetings don't last long!

Unfathomable questions
These are thought-provoking questions you can ask your group to ponder during their lift journey.

- So, tell me. Why are you on earth?

- Have you ever wondered what it must be like to be an ant?

- What do you think life would be like if everyone's brain was in one gigantic head?

- Have you ever wanted to fly? And if you could sprout wings, where would you go?

(Of course, these are just examples. Have fun making up your own.)

The Pavarotti Game

As soon as you enter the lift, start singing an uplifting song (Put On A Happy Face is my personal favourite) and encourage fellow travellers to sing with you. It can be any song, as long as it's something most people will know. The object of the game is to see how many people you can get to sing between each floor. A useful tip would be to download, print out and give everyone you meet a copy of the song sheets as you begin the game. If no one joins in, chances are you'll still make people smile (or even laugh) , which in my opinion, is a win!

PHYSICAL GAMES

Balance the lift

Create an atmosphere of fun by politely asking fellow passengers to move to various positions so the lift is 'balanced'. Make the first move and encourage your group to follow your example. If there are four passengers including yourself, direct one person to each corner. Three people require a triangle, and five require one in each corner and one in the middle. Offer to be the one in the middle. A really full lift will require rows. Do a head count first, (out loud, of course) then arrange your 'club'. Every time I do this, the result is hilarious. and I can guarantee everyone will leave the lift feeling happier and ready to face the day. What a gift to give someone!

To really commit to the happiness-enhancing benefits of The Lift Club, remember this oath, wherever you go:

I AGREE TO CREATE OPPORTUNITIES WHEREVER POSSIBLE TO TALK TO EVERYONE EVERYWHERE, REGARDLESS OF COLOUR, RACE OR CREED, AND TO EMPLOY LIFT STRATEGIES IN EVERY SITUATION TO PROMOTE FRIENDSHIP, GENERATE GOODWILL, AND ABOVE ALL, HAVE FUN!

We all deserve the opportunity to become 'Captain' of our own Lift Club and of course it's completely free, because you can't put a price on friendship. After all, how can one charge for spreading joy which belongs to everyone on the planet?

Feel free to get in touch and share your own Lift Club experiences via my blog, thecrankyguru.wordpress.com. After all, 'strangers are just friends waiting to happen' and you never know—the next person you meet might just change your life!

Chapter 4: Never judge the bottle by the label.

A train journey with a difference

Often, our teachers come to us dressed in the most unlikely apparel. If we are open and willing to not judge too quickly, the lessons can be valuable and surprising.

I was on a train heading into the Sydney CBD from North Sydney and decided to conduct a Lift Club social experiment with my fellow travellers. I was seated at the back of the train where the bench seats face each other, so it was the perfect setup to conduct a conversation. It's possible you consider me totally nuts given our social conventions about personal space, but I simply started talking to everyone as if they were specifically there to chat with each other. (Remember, the essence of Metaphysics is three magical little words: Act As If). So, in a big, happy voice I opened with, "Don't you think it's a shame that we have this time to spend together and yet we don't reach out the hand of friendship or even say hello to our neighbour? Don't you think we humans are weird like that?"

Amazingly, the response to my loudly expressed question was

instantaneous! To give you a visual, allow me to describe our group on this sunny Sydney morning. There were six people in the back section of the train. A young Asian woman with a child of about two. An attractive young woman of around 20 with a 'hippie' vibe, possibly an overseas traveller on holiday. (Mere summation on my part). A young man of about 25, smartly dressed in casual attire, playing with his phone. A suit-wearing, middle-aged business man of about 50 reading the Australian Financial Review, and in the far corner, a ragged-looking, rotund, unshaven and unkempt older man with a checked shirt and a thin belt tied in a knot around his waist. He appeared, on first impressions at least, to be the last person one would choose to engage in conversation.

So, who do you suppose responded first to my hypothesis? That's right! Mr 'Scruffy'! But not as you might expect. He addressed our group in a beautifully cultured English accent and eruditely enumerated the many reasons people don't speak to each other. Fear, prejudice, arrogance based on entrenched value judgements and misconceptions and the natural reserve common to many Western nations. The way he spoke, I had the distinct impression he was speaking from a personal perspective and possibly taking the opportunity to express his own frustrations at being marginalised and rejected. Had I inadvertently given him a precious gift? A golden opportunity for him to express his thoughts in our open instant forum? It appeared so. The conversation was picked up by our business man who rather grumpily espoused the view that he didn't want to talk to anyone in the morning on his way to work, because he's very busy and he just wants to read the paper. Even so, he had expressed his view candidly and although possibly against his will, contributed to the discussion anyway.

At this point, our group sprang to life and people began to speak with each other (with the exception of 'important business man' who went stoically back to his paper). The young man began an animated conversation with 'hippie girl' and the young woman with a child was talking to 'Mr Scruffy'. I watched transfixed as if a fire had been lit. A fire of collaborative communication.

And then, the unexpected. The smartly dressed young man stood up, produced a deck of cards and began performing magic tricks for everyone's entertainment! At the stop before mine, young man and hippie girl, who had resumed their conversation, alighted together. Had my social experiment actually been the catalyst for romance as well? I'd like to think so. As my station approached and I moved past 'Mr Scruffy' to the exit, he thanked me for facilitating the 'meeting'.

Such crazy fun, isn't it? And this is just one example of the happiness you can bring to others by simply striking up a conversation. Try it for yourself and see how much friendship you can manifest!

The Lift Club is open to everyone.

Chapter 5: Joy.

What is it and how can we get it?

The secret to true happiness is to live in the moment where no past or future event can colour our view of reality. We can rest there in the very nucleus of loving thought and creative ideas.

Most days as I sit quietly, I feel amazing energy coursing through my body as I'm struck by the miracle that is Life. Every part of me is joyful and active, and as I move my consciousness around as if on some crazy, exuberant road trip, I feel greeted by every atom and molecule. I sense their intelligence and their love for the tasks they have been given. And they acknowledge me, saying, "Hello Paul! Thank you for noticing how beautifully we collaborate in your service. We love you and we are here to do your bidding!" Every day, I give heartfelt thanks for the greatest joy of all—which is life—and for every breath I take, which keeps me living.

Have you ever thought about your breathing? It's not surprising if you haven't, as it's an involuntary aspect of our body's intelligence. Yet focusing on your breathing releases you momentarily from incessant troubling thoughts, and creates joyful 'space' in which you can simply 'be'. One can be lost in thought and found in 'the moment'. Whether we're aware of it or not, we're all part of 'All That Is'. Every living thing evolves and grows in capacity and potency through the stimulating effect of the higher vibration of consciousness. All That Is serves humanity in this way, just as we as human beings have the responsibility of stewardship towards the so-called lower kingdoms of animal, vegetable and mineral.

To express joy in our lives is the primary calling of all human beings. Furthermore, by shining a light on what is wanted in the world as opposed to what isn't, we create our happier reality and assist others around us to find theirs. We have the capacity to empower and engender growth in our brothers and sisters around the world, and I believe we're duty-bound to assist where we can. For me, joy is the outward expression of higher consciousness, residing in the Eternal Moment of Now, where only Love, the true embodiment of All That Is resides. To enter this space, we need to switch off the ego mind and engage the feeling heart, because nothing we do makes sense if we don't touch the hearts of others. When we do, joy is the result.

Joy, as a byproduct of Love, can be nurtured and developed in everyone. All it takes for irrepressible joy to be awakened, is for us to learn how to love ourselves. How? Well, allow me to introduce one of the great influences of my spiritual journey: the epochal writings of 'Mystical Man' Robert Shapiro. Find a quiet place to relax and follow his words as you learn to engage your 'Heart Energy'.

How to create Heart Energy.

By 'Mystical Man' Robert Shapiro.

Take your thumb and rub it very gently across your fingertips for about half a minute or a minute. While you do this, don't do anything else, just put your attention on your fingertips.

Close your eyes and feel your thumb rubbing slowly across your fingertips. Notice that when you do this, it brings your physical attention into that part of your body.

Now you can relax and bring that same physical attention anywhere inside your chest, not just where your heart is, but anywhere across your chest, solar plexus area or abdomen, and either generate or look for a physical warmth you can actually feel. Take a minute or two, or as long as you need to find that warmth. And when you find it, go into that feeling of warmth and feel it more, just stay with it. Stay with that feeling of warmth.

Feel it for a few minutes so you can memorise the method, and most importantly, so your body can create a recollection, a physical recollection of how it needs to feel for you.

The heat might come up in different parts of your body – maybe one time in the left of your chest, maybe another time in the right of your abdomen or other places around there. Wherever you feel it, just let it be there, don't try and move it around—that's where it's showing up in that moment. Always when it comes up and you feel the warmth, go into it and feel it more.

Make sure you do this when you are alone and quiet, not when you are driving a car or doing anything that requires your full attention. After you have done the warmth for five minutes, or as long as you can do it—relax.

Now think about this: The warmth is the physical evidence of loving yourself. We've all read about how we need to love ourselves, but this exercise creates the actual physical experience of it. The heat will tend to push everything out of you that is not of you or

supporting you. Because the heat, as the physical experience of loving yourself, also unites you with Creator Energy and generates a greater sense of harmony with all beings.

You might notice as you get better at this that your friends or other people might feel more relaxed around you, or situations might become more harmonious. Things that used to bother you or upset you don't bother you as much, because the heat creates an energy not only of self love but of harmony.

Because it is heart energy, it just naturally radiates, like light coming out of a light bulb. Remember, you don't throw the heat out even with the best of intentions. You don't send it to people. If other people are interested in what you are doing or why they feel better around you, you can teach them how to do this exercise in the way you have learned or the way that works best for you.

And the most important thing to remember is that this method of loving yourself and generating harmony for yourself creates harmony for others, because you are in harmony. Remember that this will provide a greater sense of ease and comfort in your life no matter who you are, where you are, what you are doing or how you are living your life. It can only improve your experience.

The truth is, we can be who we are in every circumstance in complete alignment, and we *can* be happy. As you experience this moment, try to imagine how it is being shared by the billions of people who inhabit this planet with us. In all its myriad forms, this moment, regardless of what life has dealt us, is shared with all others. So, be joyful and loving as often as possible in the knowledge it is being distributed equally to all. By remaining joyful and positive, we assist the entire planet.

Chapter 6: Gratitude.
Being in the moment where love resides.

"No matter where we are in this beautiful world, let's go outside now, look up at the sky, look at the trees, feel the beauty of nature, join with the energy of All That Is and rejoice in our lives and the many wonderful natural gifts that have been given to us."

One morning, not so long ago, I awoke early as I do most mornings, pulled on some shorts and joggers and ran down my front path with not a care in the world. I was in a state of bliss, having just meditated, and with a cool breeze in my face and the morning sun at my back, the world was my oyster. (Damn, I'm Jewish! I don't eat oysters!) It was a perfect summer day and the kookaburras were greeting the morning with their usual cacophony.

Nevertheless, just five minutes into my run, my right toe caught on a raised lip of concrete and I was airborne, suspended in mid-air momentarily, and on my way to the mother of all face plants! Concrete's hard (is it ever soft?) and I lay akimbo for a few moments on the ground, testing all appendages. I was happy to realise that I hadn't broken any hands or fingers—a bonus, since

I'm a keen violinist. Regardless, it soon became apparent my kneecap was not in good shape, as searing pain coursed through my right limb. I'm sure I would have been forgiven for focusing on that pain if it wasn't for the fact that I know 'what we think, we create'. (In this case, more pain!) So instead, I engaged higher consciousness and sent healing energy to the source of the problem, while repeating a healing mantra as I hobbled home.

As soon as I felt a little more stable, I hopped in the car and with some difficulty, headed for the local medical centre. When a doctor finally became available, I was so impressed with the thoroughness of the examination I received. Blood pressure, ECG, Xray. The lot. The ECG revealed I had critically high blood pressure which needed immediate attention and I was quickly medicated for it!

This was when sincere gratitude kicked in. Certainly, I had cracked my kneecap in half. But if it wasn't for this accident, I would never have known I had life-threatening high blood pressure, which is now under control. So, blessed by providence, I was truly happy to be hobbling around on a stick for weeks, knowing that a more serious problem had been addressed. As for the broken kneecap, the doctor said it would take five or six weeks to heal. I said I would heal it in two and that is what happened, because belief creates our reality.

We can choose to see the glass half full.

In truth, we are all blessed beyond measure, but even so, it appears to be human nature to focus our attention on what's wrong with things. You know, a general uneasiness that things could go pear-shaped at any moment. Perhaps it's simply the burden of modern living, or thoughts of things not done, comments made and regretted or disappointment at one's perceived situation in the world compared to others. Whatever it is, it's not a feeling one would choose to entertain, is it?

Here's what I suggest: Step outside and look at the beautiful trees and the sky with the clouds rolling by. Let a feeling of immense gratitude overwhelm you and give deep thanks for your life, forgetting all else. Some might say we're often ungrateful for what we have, but the truth is we're living on the toughest planet in the Universe and having coped with Earth school and mastered resilience and fortitude, (despite everything that's been thrown at us) we're survivors, every last one of us! So, let's put on our gowns and mortarboards, stand proudly on the dais and give thanks for all the lessons that have brought us to this time and place. We can be proud of our achievements. We've earned our degrees!

There are so many beautiful people in this world, all with heartfelt desires, wishing only the very best for everyone. And having absorbed their beautiful energy, we in turn can make kind and loving thoughts our daily focus, resisting all negativity in every form and heralding a profound awakening with which the entire world will resonate. Well, that's my dream at any rate and I believe with every fibre of my being, that one day it will come to pass.

Exercise: Write a 'thank you' letter to the Universe.

I appreciate some might respond to this suggestion with the question "Paul, why would I want to do that? After all, things aren't so great for me." My answer would be, "That may be so, but the fact is we're living and where there's life, there's always the potential for a happier outcome to manifest. It's not living in denial to dream is it? Dreams do come true—especially when we know that belief in the dream manifests our preferred reality. Let's take this opportunity to thank the universe for all the good things life has offered us, as well as the even better and happier times we have to look forward to.

So, write the letter and as you do, give thanks for all your wonderful gifts, accolades, fulfilled desires and successful accomplishments. Do this knowing that time doesn't exist and past, present and future are all happening simultaneously, so your dreams have already been granted! All that remains for you to do is give deep, profound thanks and then step back and let the universe do its work. This is the very essence of metaphysics as you "act as if".

Chapter 7: Kindness.

Understanding diversity, generosity, charity and compassion.

Are we ready to accept difference? Let's dispense with judgement of any kind and simply say, "Yes, you're very different to me, I can see that. But we can put our differences aside and learn from one another in a spirit of loving acceptance. You teach me and I'll teach you. Together we'll learn and grow closer to each other."

Having reached my 66th year on the planet, I understand how little I know and how much I can still learn. But one message that is crystal clear to me is that our purpose in life is to help others, starting with our nearest loved ones and then widening that circle to include all humanity without judgement. There are so many stories throughout history of great men and women who have done this and the potential is in all of us to be great in this way. All it takes is passion for a good cause and the will to overcome the obstacles that will inevitably be placed in our path. Obstacles that are often put there by those who think we're foolish to adopt a 'world view' of life.

There is a famous story of a meeting between the philanthropist Sir Moses Montefiore and Queen Victoria who had bestowed on him his knighthood for his amazing charitable work (which continues to this day). One day, Her Majesty asked him, "Sir Moses, exactly how much are you worth?" to which he replied, "Your Majesty, I will think on this and come back to you." When they next met, Sir Moses handed Queen Victoria a slip of paper with a sum written on it. The Queen looked at it and exclaimed, "Sir Moses, that's a very large sum indeed, but I was sure you were worth more." Sir Moses replied, "Your Majesty, this is how much I have given away, and that is how much I'm worth." For me this story encapsulates this sentiment:

If you want something for yourself, give it to someone else.

And I can't think of a better real life example of it, than this: A Jew, a Muslim and a Christian walk into a school. Sounds like the beginning of a good joke right? But it's a reality brought to fruition by Rabbi Zalman Kastel, from Brooklyn, New York who had a vision in 2002 that he could make a difference to the understanding of diversity in Australian schools. The result was his founding of Together for Humanity, (togetherforhumanity. org.au) a not-for-profit organisation that is helping schools, organisations and communities respond effectively to differences of culture and belief. You can just imagine the such a diverse group comprised of Muslims, Christians, Jews, Agnostics, Atheists, Indigenous Australians and Pacific Islanders would have on teachers, students and people from diverse backgrounds, communicating as never before in open, supportive and enjoyable school settings. What a great concept!

I have been an enthusiastic supporter of the foundation for some years now and for me, the most inspiring collaboration is between Rabbi Zalman Kastel and Sheikh Haisam Farache. On the surface, they appear to be an unlikely pairing. But the very image of them walking side by side through sometimes highly prejudiced environments as good friends, with equal respect for each other's cultures and beliefs is so very inspiring, without a word needing to be spoken. Here's what they say about their friendship and the sharing of a common cause.

Rabbi Zalman Kastel: National Director, Together for Humanity Foundation.

As a result of the work I do with Together For Humanity, I feel better about myself as a person, because I've met so many diverse, funny, interesting and inspiring people along the way. It not only brings me joy, it's allowed me to overcome my own limits and get away from prejudice. I get to see more of the world and the beauty of humanity, as well as appreciate the things I couldn't have appreciated if I hadn't been involved.

Together For Humanity does two main things. The first is that we go into schools and talk to the kids about how we can work together. We make them think about some of the prejudices and ways we see people as outsiders.

The other thing we do is to bring kids together from different backgrounds to do community service projects, like write stories for refugee children or set up car washes to help raise money for poor people in Africa. So not only do they work together to help others, play together and have fun, they also learn that no matter our differences, there are things that bring us together.

Together for Humanity has spoken with over fifty thousand children in Sydney, Mudgee, Darwin, Alice Springs, Brisbane, Melbourne—in big cities, small towns, and all around Australia. There have been times where I felt afraid, when I've been in places where people have been hostile and sometimes the kids laugh at me, but it's very rare. I remember one time, we were in a rough school—there were bars on the glass doors and it looked a bit like a zoo. The children were saying, "There's a Jew in the library! There's a Jew in the library!" and they had their faces pressed to the bars, looking in. It was like I was an animal in a big, comfortable cage.

But things like that are funny rather than scary. Later, we sat and had a great time with the kids. Some of the teachers were pretty grouchy —they'd lost hope—they didn't feel like things were ever going to get any better. I said to them, "I know what you're thinking. You think I live in a fantasy land, believing this might make a difference. But I know the real world—I know that there are people who are bigoted and hostile. But that's every bit as real as some of the students who said to me, "We need more circles like this, where we can talk to each other and respect each other." It certainly is a good step. A good start.

Sheikh Haisam Farache, Lakemba Mosque.

I am an Imam at Lakemba Mosque in Sydney, one of the biggest mosques in Australia. Together for Humanity works with three main faith organisations (Jewish, Christian and Muslim) and explores how we can realise our humanity and look past the differences and the facades that some of us may have. We speak to school children and show them that you can be strong in your faith yet at the same time accept other people because they are human beings. We discuss common themes, for example, how all people want peace, security, happiness and to be accepted for who they are, as they are. The program engages kids to get involved in their communities, some bake goods for homeless people, others play sports and raise money that helps their community. One of the fantastic things about Together For Humanity is that when you work with someone, you have to focus on a particular and common goal. Working together—especially to help someone else—takes away the insecurities and negative thoughts one may have about another. You realise that you can both contribute to achieve common goals and you begin to see the real humanity of the other person.

Since working with Together For Humanity, the light inside of me is considerably brighter. I think that the rigidness I had about my own faith, because of my own insecurities, has decreased. Sometimes, there are those little blocks, the kind of insecurities that we may have about ourselves and what people think about us. I vehemently believe in and practice my faith, but I'm firmer in my faith because of the diversity of people I've met.

For example, I traveled with Rabbi Zalman Kastel to Darwin. He wanted to cook something, but in order to make his pan kosher, he had to wash it in a natural body of water, like the ocean. I found this practice to be a lot stricter than my own Muslim faith but at the same time, it was encouraging. I thought, "Wow! Zalman practices his faith and does so irrespective of what anyone else thinks." It's definitely reinforced my own faith, because other than Muslims, I had never seen anyone that adherent and fervent about worshipping God. It was refreshing.

As Muslims, we pray five times a day. Before meeting Zalman, I might have been a little careful where I prayed and maybe delayed it in case I got harassed because I don't want to put myself in that situation. Now, I don't mind people seeing me pray, as long as I'm in a safe environment.

By interacting with thousands of Australians from different cultural and racial backgrounds, I had an epiphany. I came to a realisation about my own humanity; that as a Muslim, God wants me to actualise my humanity through my faith.

A note on compassion

As I walked to Golders Green shops for a coffee, on a recent holiday in London, I encountered a derelict man violently kicking a bin as his unfortunate partner begged him to stop. I didn't intervene as the situation was so volatile. But on my way back, I saw him sitting on the footpath and stopped to speak with him. He found my presence calming, and told me his story of anger and booze and living rough, with his poor partner in absolute despair. I told him I could see the good person inside and encouraged him to listen to his partner (she held three degrees) and seek help. He thanked me and said after meeting me he would try to be less angry. The world is full of good people who just need a little understanding and support. The next morning, I saw them again, sitting on a seat at the bus stop with their belongings beside them and I greeted them warmly like old friends. I don't know where they are today, or what destiny has in store for them, but we must always consider *there but for the grace of God...*

"Judge not lest ye be judged" is a Universal Truth of profound insight and yet it seems the penny for many has not yet dropped. In wanting to teach others hard lessons, (usually from a position of elevated 'rightness') WE become the recipient of the very same lesson! We may feel wronged and want to teach others in a harsh manner, however it will teach nothing but harshness, which is then reflected backward *and* forward! If we were breathing our last breath on earth, would we want this to be our legacy? Our contribution to humanity? I think not.

A note on charity

One afternoon, there was a gentle knock at the front door. On opening it, I was greeted by two nicely dressed, young Jehovas Witnesses with the 'Good Book' in their hands. They introduced themselves to me as Greg and Celeste, "And we're here to share a scripture reading with you," they said. "Wonderful," I replied. "Please come in, sit down and tell me your message." Celeste read a short passage ending with the words "And you will have eternal Life." "Terrific!" I said. "Thank you for sharing this with me." (I knew about eternal life already of course, but chose not to complicate their zeal with my esoteric understanding). I asked them if they had ever been invited in like this before, to which they replied "No, never." They asked if they could call on me again. I said, "Certainly, but if it's not me opening the door, run!"

It occurred to me later, that my two young bible friends Greg and Celeste were much like Brad and Janet in The Rocky Horror Picture Show. As they knock on doors, protected by their rock-solid faith, but still pristine and untarnished by deeper awareness, they walk the narrow path of beliefs that nevertheless create their reality. We all do this without exception. There is no end to deeper understanding and awareness. It's a fathomless journey of discovery, as every new door is opened to us. Behind each door regardless of its colour or condition, rich new adventures await with endless potential for emotional and spiritual growth. So I say to Greg and Celeste, keep knocking! Expose yourselves to the magical kaleidoscope of eclectic Life. Some of it is bound to rub off!

A note on compliments

Don't you think it would be wonderful if every day, we payed a perfect stranger a compliment? For example, I walked up to a heavily-tattooed biker once and said, "Nice tats." He replied, "Thanks mate," and a little more positive energy was added to the planet. Regardless of our religious beliefs or whatever spiritual disciplines we may follow, we can ask for all impurities of mind and body to be lifted from us at any time, and replaced by the qualities of heartfelt Love and Compassion. Let's transcend mind and 'think with our hearts'—the compassionate hub of our existence. Regardless of our perceived position in the world, we can all live exemplary lives. Let this be our benchmark of success, not the trappings of wealth and power.

I'll end this chapter with a demonstration of the 'compassionate hug'. You may ask why would I include a hug? Well, it makes perfect sense in the context of kindness. There is well-documented research that shows hugging and laughter are extremely effective in contributing to the healing of sickness, loneliness, depression, anxiety and stress—especially where the hearts are pressing together. A nurturing hug builds trust and a sense of safety, while boosting oxytocin levels, which heal feelings of loneliness, isolation, and anger. In addition, holding a hug for an extended time lifts your serotonin levels, elevating mood and creating happiness. Here's how to do it:

The Compassionate Hug in two simple steps

1. As the 'hugger', approach the 'hugee' with arms outstretched. (This way, it is obvious you are hugging and not shaking hands).

2. Rather than approaching front on, turn your body so that you consciously place your heart over their heart. This creates beautiful, non-verbal 'heart to heart' communication, while giving profound meaning to your compassionate intent.

We can all live compassionately, simply by recognising the heart and soul in others.

Chapter 8: Mentors.

Neil Glasser MVO, and my dad, Cecil George Bennett.

There are people born into this world who will simply not take 'no' for an answer. My friend and mentor Neil Glasser was such a man who lived by the mantra "If you want to get things done, don't ask!"

Neil Glasser, born 1918. The lesson: Audacity.

My friend and mentor of over thirty years, Neil Glasser, lived the kind of life from which legends are made. Now 94 and retired from the thrust and parry of commercial life, his star will always burn bright in my heart and mind. I will never forget the enormous influence he had on my life and the many lessons he taught me through some of the exciting adventures we shared together. Neil was dynamic and extremely charismatic and considered by many to be a genius in the art of promotion—self and otherwise!

"Don't worry Paul, it's just a blip."

Little did I know, that fate was about to throw Neil and me together in dramatic and life-changing ways. Business had been brisk in the heady excesses of the '80s, and the advertising agency, I ran with Tutti, The Bennett Creative Group, was travelling well. We were making good money and had opted to place a substantial amount of it in 'Key Man' insurance. Three years later, life had turned decidedly pear-shaped for us. An ill-considered business deal found us tottering on the brink of bankruptcy. It was then we discovered all the money we had invested in the insurance policy had gone straight into the pockets of our agent! There was no nest egg and we were in dire straits.

It was then that a good friend, Anthony, suggested I engage his Uncle Neil to assist us in our time of need. But what could Neil do? We had already exhausted all the normal channels and found out that what the agent had done was legal at the time. I met with Neil and told him of our dilemma. Neil smiled (in fact, he was always smiling!) and said, "Don't worry Paul, it's just a blip!"

And so, for the first time of many to follow, I watched the master at work. The next day we arranged to meet at the head office of the offending insurance company without an appointment. I arrived early and waited in the opulent reception area. Soon after, the lift doors opened and in walked

Neil, dressed immaculately in a beautiful, grey-striped suit with matching white shirt and tie. He looked every inch the fabulously wealthy and successful entrepreneur he was. We shook hands and he said quietly, "Follow me, Paul." Without another word, Neil walked straight past the beautifully-groomed receptionist, into the body of the office. What audacity! What bare-faced fearlessness! Then, he simply chose an empty office and told me to "wait here", as he went in search of the Managing Director.

My heart was pounding, but I knew I was being assisted by a 'business angel' with only my best interests at heart. Shortly afterwards, Neil returned with the Managing Director who listened with some compassion as I poured out my grief. The result was, the agent was compelled to give us at least some percentage of our money back, straight out of his own pocket. Neil used to say to me, "Paul, if you want to accomplish anything, DON'T ASK! Just do it and you can always apologise later!"

His other great lesson was, "Always deal with the boss, with the decision maker." Unfortunately, our world is full of pessimists, always ready to say why things aren't possible. Neil showed me what supreme positivity looks like, and just what could be accomplished if we are prepared to take a chance. Some time into my relationship with Neil, his nephew, my friend Anthony, passed away after fighting cancer for many years. Neil decided to make an album in his honour and raise money for the Spastic Centre (now called the Cerebral Palsy Alliance), of which he was a supporter. I was delighted to contribute my design skills to the project, producing the CD cover and a small booklet explaining the tracks, with a tribute to Anthony inside.

Not long after the album was released, Neil called me and said, "Paul, you've been a big help to me, and I'd like to repay you for your generosity. How would you like to travel with me to America?" Well, I was gobsmacked, but after discussing it with Tutti, I decided to embrace this amazing opportunity and so began one of the great adventures and growth experiences of my life.

The adventure begins.

Neil had arranged for us to visit San Francisco, Los Angeles and New York, so you can imagine my excitement as we set off on this amazing journey. Even though Neil was in his 70s at the time, my overriding impression of him was of a man with an incredible zest for life, expressed through unbridled interest.

By that, I mean *everything* seemed of interest to him. Produce in supermarkets, the meat window in Woolworths, anything to do with packaging and everything to do with promotion. His enthusiasm was infectious and I began to realise that Neil lived in the moment, enjoying and exploiting every opportunity presented to him. In every city, we stayed at the Hilton. Neil knew everyone and was greeted with great warmth everywhere we went. I felt that I was in school, learning the finer points of networking and marketing. Neil was constantly inquisitive, asking questions of strangers and seeking opportunities that would otherwise not be available.

I recall being in a lift with Neil in San Francisco. It was full of suited businessmen and no sooner had the lift doors closed than Neil engaged everyone present in conversation. He introduced himself as a businessman from Australia and proceeded to give the best lift talk I'd ever heard. In no time at all, he knew what everyone did and then started to make business suggestions, exchanging cards with several of them. I think it's fair to say that travelling with Neil was never dull!

One day we were walking down O'Farrell Street, not far from the Hilton Hotel in San Francisco, when we passed what appeared to be a BMW car launch event. Looking through the glass windows of the showroom, we could see that everyone was wearing evening dress and looking ever so sartorial, while we looked very much like the rumpled tourists we were. "Paul, let's get a drink," said Neil, and he headed for the front entrance with me in tow. Once there, Neil approached the security guards and, flashing a business card with his picture on it and the title *Neil Glasser MVO Journalist, Brisbane Courier Mail*, he said to them, "Boys, we're here to do a story on the new car." Well, they let us in! The only thing real about that card was the MVO, (Member of the Royal Victorian Order) which Neil had received from his friend Queen Elizabeth II for his services to the crown as promotions manager of the Queen Victoria Building in Sydney, but that's another book entirely! Anyhow, we were enjoying a quiet glass of Shiraz when security finally twigged and courteously ushered us out again. What great fun!

A life lesson.

It was April 1992 at approximately 6:45 pm, the night before our departure for Los Angeles. Neil and I sat watching the TV and the news was bleak. The Los Angeles riots were in full catastrophic melt down. We looked at each other in silence, neither of us daring to broach the obvious. Finally, Neil spoke the eight words which have resonated through my mind ever since. He said, "Paul, if we don't go, we'll never know." It was a life lesson I've always remembered. The next day, we boarded our plane for war torn Los Angeles.

Into the war zone.

As we approached LA International Airport, the pall of smoke hanging over the city looked ominous. I was amazed by how safe I felt travelling with my 75-year-old companion, who incidentally, had only recently recovered from a triple bypass operation. At the time, I remember thinking that Neil was invincible and certainly not because of any physical attribute. It was his unshakeable self-belief and an indomitable will that made him irresistibly charismatic to so many. Walking out of the airport, the smoke looked even thicker on the ground and the place was practically deserted, except for a line of twenty travellers stretching towards one lone, yellow taxi.

"We'll never get out of this airport!" I thought to myself, but Neil had other ideas. Without a moment's hesitation, he brazenly walked to the head of the line, talked briefly to the cab driver and beckoned for me to follow him. Walking past all those people in the same predicament was difficult indeed, but in moments, we were in the cab and on our way to the Los Angeles Hilton. To this day, I don't know how Neil pulled that one off, but this was my mentor Neil Glasser MVO, a most amazing man!

Mentor: Cecil George Bennett: 1916 - 1975
The lesson: Tenacity.

I give thanks for my beautiful, creative father, who in his gentle way, taught me to paint and set the course of my life. What a blessing he was.

Now for a mentor story with a different dynamic entirely. Mentoring as we know, can come in many guises and when we least expect it. Of course, every one of us can find ourselves in the role of mentor—to our family and friends, and even complete strangers. I'm finding it quite cathartic writing this story of my dear father and I feel as if I should just pour out my love for him onto these pages and let you, dear reader, make of it what you will.

There is sadness also, since I lost my dad so early—he was only 59 when he passed away. And yet he had a profound influence on my life. Where Neil was rambunctious, brazen and audacious, Dad was the exact opposite. A 'gentle gentleman', quietly spoken with a sweet manner and a prodigious talent for drawing and painting. I loved watching my dad create his art and it seemed to me that he mentored me without the need for dialogue at all. He taught me by example, by living an exemplary life, working hard to support my mother, Ray, my brother David, and me.

From an early age, Dad was afflicted with a bad stammer which severely limited his ability to speak in public. When occasions called for him to address a crowd, it was very difficult for him, such was his acute embarrassment when words were hampered by his impediment. Regardless, he would not let this obstacle stand in his way. One of my proudest moments was when he 'spoke' at my Bar Mitzvah. A Bar Mitzvah is a young Jewish boy's right of passage, a coming of age from boyhood to manhood at the age of thirteen.

How could a proud father not express his love for and pride in his son on an occasion such as this? Dad was in a quandary. He knew if he spoke publicly, his message would be lost and his speech would be about his impediment. Still, where there's a will, there's a way and Dad certainly had the will and the tenacity to find a solution to this dilemma.

After a Bar Mitzvah, there's usually a big party thrown for friends and family. Mine was held at the home of my grandparents Norman and Lydia Fox, for about eighty people. Every family member and dignitary from our small Brisbane community was there, and after a delicious fish meal prepared by my grandmother, (who caught all the fish herself) it was time for the speeches. Rabbi Fabian spoke first and as a professional public speaker, his address was eloquent and polished. He was followed by the president of our synagogue, John Lipski, who prided himself on never using notes and just speaking from the heart, ad lib. And then it was Dad's turn.

He rose from his seat and moved to the podium. As we watched, he set up a tape recorder and with a big smile towards me and our guests, pressed the 'play' button. What ensued was his speech to me, still hesitant, but having recorded it in the calm environment of his studio, he was able to say exactly what he wanted to say, and express his love and pride in my accomplishment of becoming a man that day. It was a 'wow' moment I will never forget as long as I live. I couldn't have been more proud of the way in which he overcame adversity. The lesson was learned. Tenacity. Never give in or lose sight of the dream, because all is possible.

There were other stories of Dad's tenacity around his early days as an illustrator. Dad had gone to university and studied to be a dentist, his father's profession, but his prodigious artistic ability was so obvious that he soon decided to change careers and become an artist. In the 1940s, illustration was greatly favoured in newspapers and magazines, and Dad decided he would like to be an illustrator for the Brisbane Courier Mail. But first, he needed to get an interview and since his stammer made phoning virtually impossible for him, especially when he was nervous, he decided to just go in and sit in their reception until an interview was granted. As the story goes, he simply sat there every day for weeks, until finally in exasperation, the editor said, "OK Bennett, show us your work." After that, Dad illustrated the front covers of the Courier Mail for many years to come.

Despite being two very different men, there's an interesting parallel between Neil Glasser MVO and my dad Cecil George Bennett: audacity and tenacity! One with the 'gift of the gab' and the other with no gift for that at all, but each living their lives and making the best of their talents. I love you Dad. Rest in peace. Incidentally, Dad had a good friend and client John McCann, who shared the same speech impediment, but approached the challenge very differently. His view was, "OK, I know this is going to take a while and I'll struggle to get the words out, but you can bloody well be patient and I'll get there eventually!" I'm sure he was one of Dad's greatest mentors.

Chapter 9: How to manifest your preferred reality.

The Cranky Guru talks metaphysics.

I'm happy to accept the moniker of 'insane super optimist', spouting ideas which sound completely naive and unrealistic to many, but we always have two choices. One is to see the world as we perceive it to be and 'react' to that. Or, we can dream a better world into existence. I choose the latter. I choose the dream.

We'll move slowly through this chapter. Not so slowly that you fall asleep, I hope, but slowly enough so the principles I'm introducing have time to merge with your existing ideas. Now, ask yourself this: How do people manifest their desires? Of course it would be correct to say, "Have a plan and work your butt off!" Or, as a friend of mine once advised, "Just bite off more than you can chew, and chew like hell!" There's nothing wrong with either of these concepts of course, but there's so much more going on as we engage the universe in our plans. After all, the universe *is* engaged, whether we realise it or not!

I'd like to make it clear from the start that the techniques, and philosophies espoused in this chapter are my own personal beliefs, inspired by the channelled wisdom of many Masters over more than thirty years. However, these principles of manifestation are readily available to all and through this book, I'm simply wanting to give a wider audience the opportunity to judge the effectiveness of these beliefs in their lives, for themselves.

Let's consider the concept of time.

Without getting too technical, here are a few basic ideas. Time is a dimension in which events can be ordered from the past, through the present into the future. It's also the measure of durations of events and the intervals between them. Some simple, relatively uncontroversial definitions of time include 'time is what clocks measure' and 'time is what keeps everything from happening at once.'

Time has long been a major subject of study in religion, philosophy and science, but defining it in a manner applicable to all fields without circularity has consistently eluded scholars. Nevertheless, diverse fields such as business, industry, sports, the sciences, and the performing arts, all incorporate some notion of time into their respective measuring systems. (Essential really—just imagine trying to catch a bus or plane without time! How difficult would that be?)

Now, ask yourself this: What makes something 'real'? We humans usually decide what's real by using our five senses of sight, smell, taste, touch and hearing. But can any of our five basic senses detect time? The answer is no. Time only exists in a relative sense and if we are to fully understand and use metaphysics in our lives, we must accept that time doesn't exist.

Here's the hypothesis:

If we accept that time is not 'real', shouldn't we accept that the linear progression of time is also not real? Meaning, everything we've thought of as past or future is really happening *now*. Just stop whatever you're doing for a moment, stretch your arms out to the sides and imagine every meaningful thing that's ever happened in your life moving forward in line with your arms, instead of behind you. So, everything that ever happened in your life can be revisited. Re-lived! That's how I understand timelessness.

To take this idea even further, if our 'arms' demonstration has helped us understand all past happenings as being simultaneous, then so too are all 'future' happenings. Meaning, everything that could possibly happen based on our thoughts, words and actions has already happened in probable reality. This is not so crazy. After all, don't elite athletes visualise themselves winning the race, jumping higher, throwing further? The only difference between what their coaches and motivators are telling them and what I'm telling you now, is that the visualisation—the great dream—is *actually* happening now, in a parallel, probable reality. It's parked, just waiting to be 'real-ised'. Our role is simply to align our passion, energy, will, desire and (most importantly) our absolute belief, to manifest this desired 'probable' outcome in our waking 'now' reality.

Consider this analogy. You're watching your favourite TV program, while your other favourite is playing simultaneously on a parallel station. Add to this countless dramas, comedies, news events, music shows and soap operas, all playing at once on different stations. This is a picture of human consciousness. We humans, being linear in our thinking over millennia, can only 'tune in' to one station (one reality) at a time, but it doesn't mean all the other programs aren't equally 'real'. However, we *can* choose another station simply by changing what we think. Because, "what we think, we create!"

The main principles of timelessness:

1: We are not imprisoned in time, unless we think we are.

We are multi-dimensional beings living multi-dimensional existences. All our probable pasts and futures are happening now and changing all the time with every thought, word and action. So, what does this revelation mean? It means we need have no regrets. We simply keep creating better and better versions of ourselves, and as we do, everything changes in the eternal moment of now. That's a comforting thought isn't it?

2: What we think, we create.

Although a car will take us where we want to go, our deeper understanding of how to 'drive thought' will take us so much further. This is the vehicle we need to master. Every thought creates a probable reality. We are often so cavalier in our thinking, unconscious of the fact that we are creating every instant. Surely it's true that if you think something can't be done, it can't? For many, reality is unfairly harsh, since we so often choose to think and fear the worst. Your chances of success are much greater if you 'consciously' think only those thoughts you want to see manifest in your physical reality. You need to focus exclusively on positive outcomes, knowing deep in your heart that they have already been created! For instance, you might think, "Will I turn left or right? I'll turn left." But as you act on this thought, 'right' has also been simultaneously created as a probable reality, needing nothing more than your action to become a physical truth. This is how gossamer thin the veil between what we're living and what we *could* be living really is. Every thought is an act of Creation. It is a case of 'sliding doors'.

3: Thoughts, being energy, cannot be destroyed.

Where do our thoughts go? They may have disappeared from our memory in a blink, but they're still out there, doing what thoughts do. If we could follow them and track their paths of healing, loving or otherwise, perhaps we'd think twice before creating them in the first place. Or, in finally understanding their awesome power, wouldn't we choose to create more of some and less of others?

I was discussing this idea with a friend recently and he said, "But there's so little electricity in a thought, how can it have any impact?" to which I replied, "Not electricity, but units of consciousness." You may think I'm speaking solely of the 'mental apparatus, but the effect of thought is much deeper. Every atom and molecule in our bodies is impacted by thought, and responds instantly.

A perfect example?

We've all had the experience I'm sure where a well meaning friend looks intently at you and says, "You're looking very tired today." Result? You immediately feel tired, even if you were feeling perfectly fine a moment before. Why? Because our very physiology has changed. We have taken on the intent of the thought. Now, we all know—and every physicist will confirm—that nothing is really solid. Everything is made of atoms and molecules moving at amazing speed to create the shape, look and feel of physical things, including us. These atoms and molecules have intelligence and consciousness. How could they not, being able to collaborate so perfectly with each other? So, although we may be looking at what appears to be a solid object, what we are really observing is constant change created primarily by our thoughts and beliefs.

Exercise: How to overcome tiredness.

This method of overcoming tiredness may sound simplistic, but I've found it to be profoundly efficatious. Here's the scenario: You've had a long, hard day and yes, your energy levels have taken a battering. However, what we all tend to think in this moment is the very thing not to! We say to ourselves, "I AM really tired." I've placed the words "I AM" in caps, because in case you don't know it, they are the two most powerful words in the english language and the cosmic initiators of our individual reality, no less! So, they are the very words to help us in our diminished condition and using our newly discovered cosmic initiators, we say instead. "I AM refreshed" or, "I AM rested" or, "I AM energised." In my experience, the effect on my entire physiology is instantaneous!

Please try this and let me know of your experience on my blog thecrankyguru.wordpress.com. Trust me, it works!

Chapter 10: The 'Belief' Principle.

How your beliefs create your reality.

'Manifestation' is a big, grandiose word conjuring up images of super-hero-like exploits and accomplishments, but the reality is, *every* thought and belief we have manifests an outcome of some kind. They determine the nature of what we see. Quite literally, we see what we want to see. We see our own beliefs and emotional perceptions materialised in physical form and if we desire change in our experience, then it is necessary for our beliefs and attitudes to change first.

This is where an understanding of the 'rules of manifestation' becomes most useful. Not one thing in the entire universe has any meaning except the meaning we give it and as such, we are the ultimate creators of our physical reality.

Let me tell you a story. Many years ago, before I'd met my wife Tutti, I went to the movies with Estelle, my girlfriend at the time. As the movie ended and we were about to go for coffee, I experienced a profound sense of foreboding which appeared before me in the shape of a dark, grey cloud. In this moment, my over-riding belief was one of impending violence. This experience completely changed my game plan and I said to Estelle, "Let's not do coffee now, if you don't mind. I think I'll just drive you straight home." Which is exactly what I did. We had a coffee together at her place instead, I kissed her goodnight and headed for home.

I'd been travelling for no more than five minutes, when I reached an intersection with the green light in my favour and I proceeded across. Instantly, the blinding glare of a truck's headlights blocked my vision and a drunk driver who had run the red light, slammed into my car door, rolling my car four times. I suffered a punctured lung and seven broken ribs. The ambulance men cut me out with the 'jaws of life' and I was very lucky to survive.

So, what's the point of my story? Well, my premonition completely changed my belief, and the action I then took, quite obviously placed me in harms way. There's a big 'what if' here isn't there? What if I had disregarded my negative feelings, engaged a more positive view and gone for coffee with Estelle as originally planned? Could I have saved myself a truckload of pain and months of recovery? It's impossible to know for sure, but the point is this: changing our belief about things changes our approach, and then our world changes irrevocably. That's how powerful we are. (No pressure though!) But rather than just hypothesising, can we actually prove our beliefs create our reality? I believe we can.

Can we prove our beliefs create our reality?

Let's suppose a child has been born into a family whose father just happens to be head of the Ku Klux Klan. This unfortunate child will be schooled from birth in the dangers of associating with practically anyone who does not fit the white supremacist belief system. These beliefs will then colour every aspect of this young person's life, as if viewing the world through tinted lenses. And this will remain the reality until such a time as something happens to modify those beliefs. As the beliefs change, so too will the reality.

The Irrevocable Universal Law.

I've managed to reduce the entire discipline down to just three words: 'act as if'. This is the very essence of metaphysics and the bedrock of esoteric manifestation as I understand it. However, what we must accept first of all if we are to effectively engage these principles, is to totally accept the following:

1) Time does not exist.

2) What we think, we create.

3) Our beliefs create our reality.

4) Past, present and future are all happening simultaneously.

Now, it might seem obvious, but there is a big difference between our desires—those things we want—and our beliefs. We all 'want' certain things in our reality, but if we do not actually believe they are possible, should we be at all surprised if they don't manifest?

To fully embrace our true potential, we must disregard all beliefs which imply limitation of any kind. These beliefs can be very sneaky and well hidden. So, we need to find them and eliminate them. They may be beliefs instilled in childhood by domineering, albeit well-meaning parents, for instance. There are so many stories of parents who, for whatever reason, treated their children harshly—even cruelly—undermining their self-esteem and convincing them they are worthless.

If this did in fact happen, the actual incident may well be forgotten, but the belief of 'not good enough' may still remain lurking in the shadows, colouring every effort and every attempt at personal success. Quite obviously, we would not choose to harbour beliefs such as these, and they can be set adrift!

Are you brave enough to analyse your beliefs?

As I've said, many of our beliefs have been 'super-glued' to us by religion, culture and major life events, but if we are honest with ourselves, we may accept they are creating a barrier to our happiness. No one can experience for us what we as individuals feel and believe, regardless of the good advice gained through listening to gurus, ministers, psychologists and friends. We can't be 'told' what to believe by others, even with the best intentions, since the deepest and most profound understanding will always come from within.

Belief in self is essential and we can harness both our intelligence and consciousness in equal measure to make correct personal decisions free of coercion of any kind. It is our right.

If we accept that beliefs are the bedrock of creation, manifesting our reality, it makes sense to sift through the 'back catalogue' of our core beliefs, discarding those that no longer support us and replacing them with ones that do. In my view, this is the best way to break an unwanted cycle and afford real change.

How to change your beliefs in four easy steps.

Step 1: Find a quiet space away from all distractions and start by writing down what you consider to be your core beliefs. Ask yourself questions like 'What am I afraid of and why?' 'Do I like people?' 'Am I likeable?' and so on. Do this fearlessly and honestly and don't shy away from the tough questions such as 'Do I judge people?' or 'Am I prejudiced?' The most important thing while doing this exercise is not what you *think* about your answers, but how you feel. It's possible that some statements may bring up deep emotion. Put a tick next to those for further analysis later on.

Step 2: Once you have gone through your core belief list as thoroughly as possible and ticked those beliefs you would like to change, sit quietly and think deeply on them one at a time. This is not a meditation and no technique of any kind is required. You're just having a quiet chat with yourself in the understanding that change is necessary and it can be achieved by eliminating those beliefs that are creating limitations.

Step 3: It's important now to accept the old belief as yours and then just say: "This belief is no longer useful to me and I now eliminate it from my thinking. I now believe I AM (insert the new belief here)." Sometimes these new beliefs will require some reinforcement and so repetition is necessary. Just keep repeating "I AM..." until you feel totally comfortable with it and then watch the magic happen!

Step 4: Now, beginning with the magical words "I AM", you can also tell yourself how great you feel, how enthusiastic, charismatic, fearless, young, slim, and beautiful you are, as well as healthy, happy AND successful! Using this technique, I've found I can 'rest' in my beliefs and gather them around me like familiar old blankets. Then, feeling clearly what's not comfortable or helpful, simply throw them off or replace them, like unnecessary layers on a hot summer night.

Can you create the reality of youth? Of course you can!

One morning, as I visited my 94 year old mum at the home, she greeted me at the door with a comb in her hand. "Paul, your hair looks terrible!" She said. "You're a mature man. How can you stand to get around like that? It's a disgrace!" I thought for a moment and then the penny dropped. I had forgotten to tell Mum

I had recently manifested the age of 20 in my consciousness. That would have explained everything! Not to mention the fact that now I'm twenty again, I'm my wife Tutti's toy boy!

How good is that?

Sometimes, I'd hand mum a brush and mirror so she could comb her hair and put on some lipstick. She'd look in the mirror and shake her head in disbelief and say, "Who is that old woman?" Of course, when we contemplate the infinite capacity of the human mind, with so much potential as yet undiscovered and unused, it's little wonder we are perplexed by the human predisposition to age and lose physical function. Surely it's not necessary?

In biblical terms, Moses was 120 years old when he died. "Yet his eyes were not weak nor his strength gone." Now, I am not meaning to value youth over old age in a narcissistic sense, but for the singular purpose of keeping our bodies in top physical working order. Of course, it wouldn't hurt to look a little better for longer, would it? We simply do not need to grow old, tired and listless.

And at the very least, by thinking 'young', coupled with a healthy diet and exercise, (both scientifically proven to boost longevity) we can greatly slow down the ageing process. As I've said so often in this book, our beliefs create our reality, not just in a mental sense, but in an actual physical sense as well, and every last one of us can prove it for ourselves. But first, we must change our understanding of time by accepting it doesn't exist, believe deeply that our beliefs create our reality and revise our core beliefs where necessary to affect the changes we desire. It's not so hard once you get the hang of it!

Can I prove this? Well, I've chosen myself as the guinea pig for this experiment, and having already manifested the age of twenty in my consciousness, we may have to wait a few years to really see the ultimate benefits.

My daily visualisation for ongoing youth.

This is my personal daily visualisation which has kept me young and fit all these years. Of course, it's based on unshakeable belief and knowing that every cell in my body is there to afford healing, harmony and balance. I breathe in deeply, and as I do, I visualise all my cells as pulsating circles of healing light, working seamlessly together to fix any health issues, while removing all impurities with every outward breath. So with eyes closed, I breathe in and out until I feel totally refreshed. Please try it and let me know if this works for you too.

Can you lose weight? Of course you can!

Using the principles of manifestation we all now understand, you can improve practically every aspect of your life. Of course you can't grow new limbs, but with regard to your weight, reducing it is a cinch! A simple example? Rather than being overweight because we eat too much, we eat too much because we believe we are fat! Change the belief and you conquer the problem. So, if you 'believe' you are thinner, you will automatically eat less! Worth a try isn't it?

Can you change the past? Of course you can!

At the very least you can feel better about the past. Accepting that your beliefs create your reality means you can change future outcomes by simply choosing to believe something else. And by accepting there is no time but simply the eternal moment of now, it is possible to change the 'past' by also choosing to believe something else. You can rewrite past errors and hurts by manifesting a different probable reality, thus removing the 'shackles' that have weighed so heavily on you in your life.

In truth, we should all do what we honestly believe is best for us, even if it is not construed that way by others. This being the case, and having created multiple 'probable realities' along the way, there's no need to go back because there's no 'back' to go to. There's just NOW. Since our beliefs create our personal reality, we can simply choose another probable outcome in our consciousness to 'rewrite' what happened and change our present situation closer to our ideal. Yes, I know this may sound crazy given our present understanding, but that's how I see it.

In every past event in our lives, even the worst possible ones, there were probable outcomes that were better and not acted upon, but regardless, they did happen in a probable reality.

Here's a useful exercise.

Let's choose a profound experience from our lives and view it differently, from the perspective of a protagonist for example. Rewrite their actions and visualise the preferred outcome: the one we would have liked to experience. This may be cathartic, but it may also provide a broader understanding of our attitudes and beliefs.

Take a moment to sit quietly and visualise that defining moment that has never been forgotten or forgiven. It could be an error made or some hurt caused by another (perhaps a parent, friend or teacher). Visualise it again and by concentrating intently, change what happened to the best possible outcome. Embrace this as the new reality, while completely 'letting go' of the old one. Give love while reflecting quietly. Forgive and be forgiven.

Of course if we prefer, we can simply view this as some crazy 'probable reality' mind game, because for some of us this may seem too far-fetched, stretching the envelope just a little too much. I totally understand, but I also know that by anchoring the principles of manifestation firmly in place, we can have a go at absolutely any adventure.

Are dreams real? Of course they are!

Many of us think that only what we see with our conscious mind is 'real', but what about what we see in our 'unconscious' sleeping state? While we're awake we're using our outer mind. But while we're sleeping, we're using the inner mind, unfettered by physical reality. We fly, we meet people, converse and learn. And we're shown things that have great meaning for us as we 'view' them.

Recently in the dream state, I was shown three very old, dusty books by a beautiful elderly gentleman. I felt I was meant to read them and so I was offered an incentive that traversed my sleeping reality. We are constantly being given assistance, regardless of whether we're asleep or awake and both realms are equally 'real' and beneficial.

It is clear to me there is a direct correlation between the creative process and dreaming. I call it 'dreaming out loud'. In other words, we bring dreamed experience into our reality as creative inspiration and in this context, dreams are far more than just pictures in the mind. They truly are, as Einstein said of imagination, "a preview of life's coming attractions" gleaned from beyond time and space.

So, dreams are not illusion. They are a vital part of our life experience, of our spiritual 'becoming' which continues unabated whether we're 'awake' or not. Only our ego mind views dreaming with a cynical eye, accepting only what can be seen in physical reality as real, while to the dreamer, waking reality is the fantasy. I believe both are equally real and important to our growth, to be explored and embraced. The reason we have such difficulty remembering dreams is that on waking, we attempt to reinterpret them from the physical perspective, when they were actually experienced in a realm where consciousness is limitless and not linear. So, when I flew silently over the impossibly irridescent green forest with the warm wind caressing my face in infinite time and space, I did.

Can you heal yourself? Yes, more than you might believe.

I heard a story recently about a man whose wife had just given birth to a premature baby girl, who needed immediate surgery for a heart defect. The surgeon came to the man and said, "As you know, your child needs this surgery, but I must tell you that her chances of surviving the operation are slim at best." The man looked at the surgeon and with a smile said, "You're fired!" "What?" said the surgeon, "You can't fire me!" To which the man replied, "Yes I can! I don't want your negative energy anywhere near my precious child!" We should never underestimate the power of positive belief. It takes strength to resist the damage caused by well-meaning pessimists!

Worry is one of the most debilitating emotions. The good news is that when you live in the moment, you have a greater chance of overcoming this potentially life-threatening condition.

Certainly, we all accept there are times when things just don't work out and we may feel worried or even depressed. However, I believe it's important to own our emotions, to embrace them and acknowledge them as our creation, then let them go.

That is to say, don't block them or deny them. Accept them. Only then can we analyse our thinking openly and honestly and establish which core beliefs led to this outcome. In truth, if we 'think little' of a perceived problem, (or not at all) it will reduce in our reality. If we magnify a problem in our minds, it will grow in our reality. Since our beliefs create our reality, it is wise to 'think carefully' and with controlled intent.

Regardless of our personal situation and the adversity we may face, we must believe the universe is with us and not against us. And as we focus on this truth with all the will we can muster, those who would help us the most are drawn to us, creating an atmosphere of mutual collaboration and growth which simultaneously benefits and illuminates a greater understanding in all contributors. Where there's a will, there's a way.

If we are candid and totally honest with ourselves, aren't there things we've denied in our lives that would actually make us truly happy? Why don't you write a list. No one else need see it.

Then, shine a brilliant light on your secret desire and manifest it in your reality. You deserve true happiness and you can make it happen. You *can* live the dream.

Chapter 11: Meditation.
A journey beyond mind.

As I meditated, I understood with crystal clarity that my reflection in the mirror was the same reflection viewed when I look at a friend or a stranger. There are no separations in reality except those we create in our minds. Surely, it makes sense then to love everyone, embrace everyone and in doing so, love ourselves even more?

As an ancient discipline, meditation assists the promotion of mental, spiritual and physical health and has been associated with the mystical branches of many major religions including Hinduism, Buddhism, Christianity, Sikhism, Judaism and Islam. Originally, the purpose of meditation was to experience increased spiritual understanding and awareness.

Since there has been so much written about meditation already, I'm keen for this book to contain my own experiences and so all the meditation disciplines shared in this chapter, I have personally practised and experienced.

Here are some methods to consider:

Every one of us has the ability to connect with higher consciousness. Although techniques are many and varied, alignment can be achieved in the most simple and direct way. Let's start with the simplest meditation of all and let's not even call it a meditation. Let's just call it 'getting in touch with Self'.

Exercise 1: Getting in touch with Self.

Find a quiet spot away from all distractions and simply sit with eyes closed. As you rest and relax, listen intently for any tones that are present. There is no right or wrong way to do this and whatever you experience is uniquely your own. The tone that you may hear is the tone of your existence, the rhythm of Life. You are simply getting in touch with your true self and being centred in 'the eternal lightness of being'. As you listen more intently for the tone, you may experience it getting louder and you may also feel a vibration connected to it. As you connect with this energy, imagine it emanating from your body and travelling in all directions, to the far reaches of the Universe, as it resonates with love and healing.

This is actually happening, since our Life Force cannot be impeded. It's the building block of creation, instrumental in forming our physical reality. I sometimes feel this vibration so strongly, it's like electromagnetic energy coursing through my body. If I'm upset about anything, this simple exercise returns me to balance again. With practice, this 'life-tone' will become readily accessible, enabling you to instantly access the 'now', while bringing you back into balance.

Some comments on Buddhist Meditation.

Meditation is a traditional Buddhist practice and although I don't want to delve too deeply into the finer technical details in this book, I would like to share this version with you. In truth, I do think it's easy to get too wrapped up in the technicalities of these practices, when meditation is really about 'being' and connecting with Higher Consciousness. It's about spaciousness and mindfulness, letting our thoughts come and go, as our breath rises and falls. In many disciplines, the breath is central to the practice and so with this next exercise, I'd like you to sit comfortably either with crossed legs, or resting in a comfortable chair in an upright position. As we feel more and more relaxed, focus on your breath. Slowly inhale and exhale, inhale and exhale.

I meditate at about 6am every morning in our lounge room on a big, comfortable couch. Personally, I think mornings are best for this when the mind is relaxed and fresh and one can focus more easily. I also think it's important to meditate in the same spot every time if possible, so that spiritual energy is built up, which will resonate throughout the entire building, turning it into a 'sacred space'.

Many people who visit Tutti and me in our home, comment on the calm and relaxing atmosphere they experience there.

Method 2: Buddhist Meditation.

It's not necessary to focus on any particular aspect of the breath, just breathe naturally and gently as you feel your body becoming more and more relaxed. Imagine you are spacious, like the clouds and the sky. As you settle further and further into a state of authenticity, let all dischord dissolve as you again connect with your fundamental nature. In Buddhist practice, this is called 'resting in the nature of mind'. As we go even further into our true nature, we connect with our authentic goodness. Loving energy is released as we feel a deep sense of peace within.

We often experience tension and anxiety in our lives as we struggle to succeed, to possess and to achieve, which is not relaxing at all. On the other hand, Buddhist Meditation brings us into a state free of all tension and concern. It is a space in which we no longer hunger to compete. A 'neutral' state, finely balanced between acceptance and rejection, hope and fear, happiness and sadness.

Often, after you've engaged a meditation practice such as this, you'll feel very inspired and creative ideas will flow freely. However, don't be discouraged if there are times when the mind is not as spacious as at others. The most important thing is to be consistent, and persevere regardless of the obstacles you may encounter. Over time, it will become easier until you can engage a 'waking' meditation, meaning you'll be able to attain a state of bliss in any situation.

Transmission Meditation.

Transmission Meditation is a form of group meditation which "steps down" spiritual energies from the Hierarchy of Spiritual Masters. Who? I hear you ask. Well, we are now moving into deeply esoteric territory, to the Ageless Wisdom Teachings of the Masters of the Spiritual Hierarchy. I've provided a full reading list at the end of this book for those of you wishing to explore the Masters further, but for now, I will say they are the Ascended Masters who have chosen to be the custodians of our planet, and assist us by sending loving, healing energy, wherever it is needed in the world. The list of Masters is extensive, but some you may be familiar with include Archangel Gabriel, Ganesh, Gautama Buddha, Isis, Jesus, John the Baptist, Krishna, Maitreya, Mary Magdalene, Archangel Michael, Moses and Vwymus.

The Ascended Masters are the custodians of all spiritual energy entering the planet, Solar, Cosmic and Inter-planetary. However, these energies are simply too high in vibration to be used directly and so transmission meditation was introduced by the Masters to assist this stepping-down process. Those choosing to form a meditation group, are allowing themselves to become 'transformers' of cosmic energy so it can be sent where it's most needed by the Spiritual Hierarchy of Ascended Masters.

This activity benefits humanity, and at the same time, accelerates the personal and spiritual growth of those who participate in the groups. All you have to do is sit peacefully with eyes closed and hold ones attention on the ajna centre, which is the point between the eyebrows, for no more than thirty minutes daily. If you feel your attention waning, then inwardly and silently, sound 'OM' to bring the attention back to the ajna centre.

Before a session is held, 'The Great Invocation' is recited by all present to invoke the energy of the Masters. This Invocation is being used by men and women of good will throughout the world in many languages. As a world prayer, it sponsors no particular group or organisation and belongs to all humanity. Here it is:

The Great Invocation *(Adapted version)*

From the point of Light within the Mind of God
Let light stream forth into human minds.
Let Light descend on Earth.

From the point of Love within the Heart of God
Let love stream forth into human hearts.
May the Coming One return to Earth.

From the centre where the Will of God is known
Let purpose guide all little human wills -
The purpose which the Masters know and serve.

From the centre which we call the human race
Let the Plan of Love and Light work out
And may it seal the door where evil dwells.

Let Light and Love and Power restore the Plan on Earth.

And there you have it!

There are more than 600 transmission meditation groups in forty countries worldwide, meeting on a regular basis.

'The Master in the Heart' Meditation.

Based on my personal experience, this is the 'grand poobah' of all meditations! It is practiced by disciples of the Arcane School, an esoteric 'house of learning' established by Alice A. Bailey in 1923 to educate serious seekers of enlightenment in the 'science of the soul'. The training in meditation techniques and overall spiritual development is conducted by correspondence through headquarters in New York, London, and Geneva. I studied for two years with an adept in London. There are no charges for the training and the work is financed through the Lucis Trust by voluntary contributions of students and others interested in serving humanity in this way.

As we've discussed, the primary purpose of meditation is to achieve alignment with soul and once this connection has been made, the desire to serve becomes almost irresistible, since the soul's singular objective is to lovingly serve humanity. So, in-depth study of this kind cannot be undertaken lightly and must be accompanied by a genuine commitment to assist the establishment of 'right human relations' on Earth.

There are several versions of this meditation, as modifications in the form are made as students progress in their study. However, this is a version more suited to the beginner. This meditation was taught by the Tibetan Master Djwahl Kuhl in the book *'Letters on Occult Meditation'* by Alice A. Bailey.

1: Alignment.

Begin by making sure you are totally comfortable and relaxed and then take three deep breaths, after which you keep the breath rhythmic and regular.

Then, visualise the three lower aspects of Man, the mental, the emotional and the physical in alignment with the overshadowing soul, while intoning the sacred word 'OM' three times for each of the three lower aspects, with the volume increasing each time. This is intended to awaken the ajna and heart centres into activity.

2: Affirmation.

Then proceed as if alignment with soul has been accomplished. (How's that for pure metaphysics?) and recite the disciple's affirmation.

"I am a point of light within a greater Light.

I am a strand of loving energy within the stream of Love divine.

I am a point of sacrificial Fire, focused within the fiery

Will of God.

And thus I stand.

I am a way by which men may achieve.

I am a source of strength, enabling them to stand.

I am a beam of light, shining upon their way.

And thus I stand.

And standing thus, revolve

And tread this way the ways of Men,

And know the ways of God.

And thus I stand."

Note: Of course, this needs to be memorised and over time will become second nature.

3: Visualisation.

You are then asked to visualise the etheric heart centre (located in the region between the shoulder blades and not the usual physical location) and picture it as a twelve-petalled golden lotus. Now, sounding the OM silently and imagining the lotus petals of love, knowledge and sacrifice slowly opening in response to this inner sound, see a radiating pool of electric blue light in the centre of which shimmers the shining jewel of soul consciousness.

With this visualisation, you have become 'open hearted' in alignment with Higher Self. Through the centre of the now fully opened lotus, build a picture of the 'Master in the Heart' as the embodiment of Higher Self. This thought form is built with loving care and attention, resonating with all the virtues and shimmering with brilliant colour and light amplified by ones love for the Master.

You have now connected with the Divine Spark, the first expression of oneself as the God within and in doing so, have simultaneously developed the ability to work with etheric, astral and mental matter.

The OM is sounded softly.

4: Meditation.

Then, move your attention to the ajna centre between the eyebrows, bringing the ajna and the heart centre into alignment in readiness for reflection on a monthly seed thought such as:

"With self-forgetfulness I gather what I need for the helping of my fellowmen."

Note: Within the Arcane school these seed thoughts are given in a progression designed to assist the student's attainment of self-forgetfulness and harmlessness in service to humanity.

5: Distribution.

Now it's time to recite The Great Invocation resonating with the energies of Light, Love and Power to awaken the higher consciousness of all humanity.

6: Conclusion.

The meditation is closed by sounding the 'OM' three times, while visualising loving and supporting energy being breathed forth into the world, strengthening the New Group of World Servers in every country as they work toward establishing right human relations throughout the whole of humanity.

One morning, when I was in deep meditation, I embraced a profound projection of my higher self. There was great, fathomless Love and understanding between us and I saw it as a symbol of the importance in our lives of unshakable belief in Self. In many respects, we are our own Master, our own Great Teacher and all we need to do is listen to our inner voice, for loving guidance to be given to us.

Chapter 12: Conclusion.

Embracing All That Is.

When we look in the mirror, our beliefs look back at us and form our image. If we see success and enthusiasm, it will be. If we see poverty and distress, this also will be. It is always our choice, as the reflection becomes our reality.

Some bright spark once said "Ask, and ye shall receive. Seek, and ye shall find." To which we said, "Thanks mate, we tried that and it didn't work!" The fact is, we may have asked, but in many cases the 'practical' mind had already decided it wouldn't, or couldn't happen. And so, we try to go ahead *and not* go ahead. Be daring *and* cautious. Brave *and* safe! The universe is really confused! It wants to give, if only we would accept, but the practical mind thinks, "I'll believe it when I see the results", while the intuitive mind says, "I'll believe NOW and the results will corroborate my belief."

So the practical mind, using rational thought to the best of its ability, harbours fears it may be wrong, while the intuitive mind 'knows' and resonates deeply with its eternal truth. The well trodden path is fearful, the other fearless. Which path will you choose to embrace? It's time now to accept these gifts. After all, you've earned them!

So, from this day forward, state clearly who you are and don't take no for an answer! You are worthy and deserving of every reward you've ever dreamed of, and now it's time to receive them! You don't have to justify your existence. You are as worthy as anyone else, so relax and enjoy the moment.

Consider this: If only we could remember the events of our previous lives, we would see how we existed in the skins of those we may now fear and despise. Surely, we'd possess a deeper understanding and trust of others, with no further need for discrimination of any kind? Having spent so much of our history focused on the physical differences of colour, culture and country, it's no surprise so many of us have entirely overlooked the most important connection of all: Consciousness. And if we could just see it, we would not judge as we do, but marvel and rejoice at our profound diversity and the multitudinous role it plays in the unification of our human family.

In conclusion, let me say this. It is my passionate belief that in time, a 'golden age' will evolve in which no man will look down on another from a different race, fully recognising the irrevocable nature of their collaboration. No gender will be considered better than another or any role in society, as each individual understands the importance of their contribution. And there will exist an open-ended consciousness linking all living beings, which will change the entire fabric of government and education to the immeasurable benefit of mankind. However, for these blessings to manifest, we must first believe they are possible.

Postscript

My journey towards understanding.

At the deepest level, we are our own teachers and physicians.

My family is Jewish, and I'm proud of this fact, particularly considering the effort my maternal grandmother, Lydia Fox, went to for us to become so. Grandma started life as a card carrying, tambourine-playing member of the Salvation Army, but when she met and fell in love with my grandfather, Norman, she made a full conversion to Judiasm, after three years of correspondence courses with the Great Synagogue in Sydney, and as far as we know, she was the first woman in Queensland ever to do so.

It was an act of extreme courage and perseverance and although she endured prejudice and objections from both families, she remained stoic in her commitment and resolve. It was definitely worth it, because she made the best *Gefilte* fish and pickled onions I've ever tasted! My mum Ray Bennett was 'fiercely Jewish' as a result of having witnessed the extreme effort her mother—my grandmother—Lydia put into her studies.

As human beings, I think we have all evolved with complex and diverse influences, attitudes and belief systems which have coloured our perspectives on life materially, emotionally and spiritually. In many ways these different views on 'what is' have created rifts and misunderstandings between us. Certainly, our adherence to various branches of faith with different commands, rules, observances and rituals have been instrumental throughout history in creating much separation and pain.

We're keen for 'our' God to be the 'One God' and so we call this personal God of ours by many different names that no doubt have deep meaning for us as individuals. But what is really needed in this crazy world is for us to come together in a deeper understanding of that which joins us so much more strongly than the things that divide us. We've spent much of our history focused on the physical differences of colour, culture and country, but none of these are anywhere near as important—as vital to humanity—as Consciousness.

If we could just see it, we would not judge as we so often do, but marvel and rejoice at our profound diversity and the multitudinous role it plays in the unification of all humanity.

Amy the Spirit Channel.

As I think back over my life, I feel there has always been a certain esoteric resonance to it. Even as a young man I was very interested in the afterlife, in spirits, the occult and the soul. And then, in the early 1970s, I met Amy, at the School of Bel Canto Singing in Brisbane. I was a young light baritone, (I'm certainly a lot heavier these days!) and Amy was a sweet-voiced lyric soprano. Everything about Amy was sweet; her voice, her personality, her plump round face and figure. I fell for her, and she became my girlfriend.

After dating for a few weeks, Amy told me she was, in fact, a spirit channel. I was very sceptical of that sort of thing in those early days, until one day she invited me to a channelling. I drove over to her house with (I must admit) some trepidation, and was met at the door by Amy who ushered me into the dining room where her mother, father and sister were already seated. As I mentioned, Amy had a high, sweet, lilting soprano voice, so just try to imagine my shock when after some obligatory deep breathing with eyes closed,

Amy finally said, "Good evening, friends!" in the deepest basso profundo and with such volume and force, I just about shot through the ceiling! This profound experience shook me to my very core and it was such a shock, that it spelled the end of our relationship. Even so, the dye had been cast and my interest stimulated.

My direction is set.

What followed was an avalanche of spiritual reading. I read everything I could get my hands on to do with the occult and esotericism, starting surprisingly with Anthony Robbins' book *Awaken the Giant Within*, followed swiftly by *The Celestine Prophecy* books one, two and three by James Redfield. These books stimulated my interest in Metaphysics and I was 'led' towards *The Game of Life and How to Play it* by Florence Scovel-Shinn, followed by her other works, *Your Word is Your Wand* and *The Secret Door to Success*.

These books had a profound influence on my interest and it was not lost on me, that every time I requested more information, the 'right' books seemed to miraculously appear, either through random comments by friends, or some chance discovery in a bookshop or on the internet.

Of course, I understand now that there is no such thing as a coincidence and I was simply getting back what I was putting out. It was around this time that I had the desire to study Buddhism and dived head first into myriad books on Indian and Tibetan mysticism. Paramahansa Yogananda's iconic books *Man's Eternal Quest* and *Autobiography of a Yogi*, introduced millions of Westerners to the teachings of meditation and with them, I became a willing devotee. I was hooked!

These books had such a profound influence on me that I wanted to share what I was learning with my wife and children. For me, the philosophies being espoused were tantamount to discovering the Holy Grail! So, let's not mince words. I became a spiritual zealot!

ZEALOT - noun.

1) *One who is zealous.*

2) *One who is full of zeal for his own specific beliefs or objectives, usually in the negative sense of being 'too' passionate; a fanatic.*

I had lost sight of the fact that 'many roads lead to Rome' and we should be gentle and accepting of those with alternate points of view, no matter how 'right' our own path appears to be.

And so, I attempted to share my profound epiphany with Tutti and the kids. To my great shock and disappointment, they hated the whole idea of esotericism and I found myself a lone voice in the wilderness. As time progressed, my obsession alienated me and moved me even further away from my loved ones. Still, the penny had not dropped and I floated on, full of altruistic zeal. I read Shogyal Rinpoche's *The Tibetan Book of Living and Dying*, plus the original *Tibetan Book of the Dead* which was composed in the 8th century by Padmasambhava, written down by his primary student, Yeshe Tsogyal, buried in the Gampo hills in central Tibet and subsequently discovered by a Tibetan, terton, Karma Lingpa, in the 14th century.

Then there was Patch Adam's book *Gesundheit* from which the movie 'Patch' was adapted. I even had the great privilege of meeting Patch as a supporter of the Australian Humanitarian Foundation of which he was patron. I became his pen pal and we corresponded back and forth with philosophic ideas for a number of years. The big shift came with the reading of Madame Helena Blavatsky's *The Secret Doctrine* and her epic tome *Isis Unveiled* in two massive volumes, *1: Science* and *2: Theology*.

These books were impossible for me to understand at the

time, but I read them anyway and after all, they did make great doorstops! Through this exposure, I was inspired to join the Arcane School run by the Lucis Trust, a non-profit service organisation incorporated in the United States in 1922 by Alice A. Bailey and her husband Foster Bailey. I studied this material online by correspondence for several years with an 'adept' based in London, including the works of Alice A. Bailey, Theosophy in general and more specifically the channelled Ageless Wisdom Teachings of the Spiritual Hierarchy of Ascended Masters.

Something had to give and quite apart from my focus being diverted from our business, cracks had begun to appear in our once idyllic marriage. No surprise there! My wife Tutti and my beautiful girls Cecily-Anna and Sonia were very unhappy and although my sincere desire to give loving assistance to humanity was spiritually fulfilling for me personally, it had generated the very opposite response in my beloved family. In fact, my altruism was seen as totally selfish and destructive and one day, Tutti came to me and said, "Paul, if we don't get professional help, our marriage is over!"

Seeking help.

This was the biggest shock of my life and the real low point in our relationship, especially since I still felt I was doing 'good works'. However, when one is a zealot, practicalities tend to take a back seat. This was over 20 years ago now, and Tutti and I have been married for 37 years. With time has come healing and a deeper understanding of who we are as two very different people. Since then, my spiritual knowledge and understanding has also deepened, to the point where I genuinely believe I can assist others to find their own path on their individual journey of becoming.

My study of this subject continued with the inclusion of the epochal writings of 'super channel' Robert Shapiro and his *The Explorer Race* series and more recently, with detailed study of the channelled writings of Seth, the internationally acclaimed spiritual teacher who spoke through the author Jane Roberts while in trance. He coined the phrase 'What you believe, you create in your reality'. This material is central to my spiritual understanding and remains the core belief of the philosophies I seek to share in this book.

I've often been told I'm a dreamer attempting to save the world, beseeching all to love humanity. But here I'll say something different. Embrace your family first! For how can we hope to love humanity if we cannot unconditionally love our own family? We can make that the first tentative step towards the greater aspiration.

References.
The literature that guided my spiritual journey.

Anthony Robbins (1986). Unlimited Power: The New Science of Personal Achievement. New York: Simon & Schuster. pp. 448 pages. ISBN 0-684-84577-6.

Anthony Robbins (1992). Awaken the Giant Within. New York: Simon & Schuster. pp. 544 pages. ISBN 0-671-79154-0.

James Redfield The Celestine Prophecy (1993) Warner Books: New York, NY ISBN 0-446-51862-X

The Celestine Prophecy: An Experiential Guide (1995) co-written with Carol Adrienne. Warner Books: New York, NY ISBN 0-446-67122-3

The Tenth Insight: Holding the Vision (1996) Grand Central Publishing: New York, NY. ISBN 0-446-51908-1

Florence Skovel-Shinn The Game of Life and How to Play It self published in 1925. "Your Word is Your Wand" published in 1928 and The Secret Door to Success published in 1940 shortly before her death on October 17, 1940

Paramahansa Yogananda Autobiography of a Yogi (1st ed.). New York: The Philosophical Library. 1946. 498 pages. LCCN 47000544 http://www.ananda.org/free-inspiration/books/autobiography-of-a-yogi/

Sogyal Rinpoche, (2002). The Tibetan Book of Living and Dying. New York: HarperCollins. p. 13. ISBN 0-06-250834-2.

Coleman, Graham, with Thupten Jinpa (eds.) (2005) The Tibetan Book of the Dead [English title]: The Great Liberation by Hearing in the Intermediate States [Tibetan title]; composed by Padmasambhava: revealed by Karma Lingpa; translated by Gyurme Dorje. London: Penguin Books ISBN 978-0-14-045529-8 (the first complete translation). Also: New York: Viking Penguin, NY, 2006. ISBN 0-670-85886-2 (hc); ISBN 978-0-14-310494-0 (pbk).

Patch Adams; Maureen Mylander (1998). Gesundheit! : bringing good health to you, the medical system, and society through physician service, complementary therapies, humor, and joy. Rochester, Vermont: Healing Arts Press. ISBN 978-0-89281-781-8. Retrieved 2008-12-16. http://patchadams.org/

Madame Helena Blavatsky The Secret Doctrine, the Synthesis of Science, Religion and Philosophy, (1888) a book originally published as two, volumes is Helena Blavatsky's magnum opus. The first volume is named Cosmogenesis, the second Anthropogenesis. It was an influential example of the revival of interest in esoteric and occult ideas in the modern age, in particular because of its claim to reconcile ancient eastern wisdom with modern science.

The Lucis Publishing Company and the Lucis Press Limited are the official publishers of Alice A Bailey's books. http://www.lucistrust.org/

Bailey's works, written between 1919 and 1949, describe a wide-ranging system of esoteric thought covering such topics as how spirituality relates to the solar system, meditation, healing, spiritual psychology, the destiny of nations, and prescriptions for society in general. She described the majority of her work as having been telepathically dictated to her by a Master of Wisdom, initially referred to only as "the Tibetan" or by the initials "D.K.", later identified as Djwal Khul.[2] Her writings were of the same nature as those of Madame Blavatsky and are known as the Ageless Wisdom Teachings

Works containing the prefatory Extract from a Statement by the Tibetan, generally taken to indicate the book was a "received" work.

Initiation, Human and Solar. 1922. ISBN 978-085330-110-3 Letters on Occult Meditation. 1922. ISBN 978-085330-111-0 A Treatise on Cosmic Fire. 1925. ISBN 978-085330-117-2 The Light of the Soul: Its Science and Effect : a paraphrase of the Yoga Sutras of Patanjali. 1997 [1927]. ISBN 978-0-85330-112-7 A Treatise on White Magic, or, The Way of the Disciple (5 ed.). 1987 [1934]. ISBN 978-0-85330-123-3 Discipleship in the New Age I. 1944. ISBN 978-0-85330-103-5 Discipleship in the New Age II. 1955. ISBN 978-0-85330-104-2 The Problems of Humanity. 1944. ISBN 978-0-85330-113-4 The Reappearance of the Christ. 1947. ISBN 978-0-85330-114-1 The Destiny of the Nations. 1949. ISBN 978-0-85330-102-8 Glamour: A World Problem. 1950. ISBN 978-0-85330-109-7 Telepathy and the Etheric Vehicle. 1950. ISBN 978-0-85330-116-5 Education in the New Age. 1954. ISBN 978-0-85330-105-9 The Externalisation of the Hierarchy. 1957. ISBN 978-0-85330-106-6 Ponder on This (compilation). 2003. ISBN 978-0-85330-131-8 A Treatise on the Seven Rays: Volume 1: Esoteric Psychology I. 1936. ISBN 978-0-85330-118-9 Volume 2: Esoteric Psychology II. 1942. ISBN 978-0-85330-119-6 Volume 3: Esoteric Astrology. 1951. ISBN 978-0-85330-120-2 Volume 4: Esoteric Healing. 1953. ISBN 978-0-85330-121-9 Volume 5: The Rays and the Initiations. 1960. ISBN 978-0-85330-122-6

Robert Shapiro, Mystical man: The Explorer Race Series: ETs & The Explorer Race Origins & the Next 50 Years Creators & Friends Particle Personalities Explorer Race & Beyond Council of Creators Explorer Race & Isis Explorer Race & Jesus Earth History ET Visitors Speak. http://plus.google. com/101684123468266008752/about<https://plus.google.com/101684123468266008752/about>

Jane Roberts (May 8, 1929 – September 5, 1984) was an American author, poet, self-proclaimed psychic and spirit medium, who claimed to channel an energy personality who called himself "Seth". Her publication of the Seth texts, known as the "Seth Material", established her as one of the preeminent figures in the world of paranormal phenomena.[1][2] The Yale University Library Manuscripts and Archives maintains a collection entitled Jane Roberts Papers (MS 1090), which documents the career and personal life of Jane Roberts, including journals, poetry, correspondence, audio and video recordings and other materials donated after her death by Roberts' husband and other individuals and organizations.[3]

Roberts, Jane (1966). How To Develop Your ESP Power. Publisher: Federick Fell. (Later retitled and reprinted as The Coming of Seth.) ISBN 0-8119-0379-6. Roberts, Jane (1970). The Seth Material. Reprinted, 2001 by New Awareness Network. ISBN 978-0-9711198-0-2. Roberts, Jane (1972). Seth Speaks: The Eternal Validity of the Soul. Reprinted 1994 by Amber-Allen Publishing. ISBN 1-878424-07-6. Roberts, Jane (1974). The Nature of Personal Reality. Prentice-Hall. Reprinted 1994, Amber-Allen Publishing. ISBN 1-878424-06-8. Roberts, Jane (1975). Adventures in Consciousness: An Introduction to Aspect Psychology. Prentice-Hall. ISBN 0-13-013953-X. Roberts, Jane (1975). Dialogues of the Soul and Mortal Self in Time. Prentice-Hall. ISBN 0-13-208538-0. Poetry. Roberts, Jane (1976). Psychic Politics: An Aspect Psychology Book. Prentice-Hall. ISBN 0-13-731752-2. Roberts, Jane (1977). The "Unknown" Reality Vol. 1. Prentice-Hall. Reprinted 1997, Amber-Allen Publishing. ISBN 1-878424-25-4. Roberts, Jane (1979). The "Unknown" Reality Vol. 2. Prentice-Hall. Reprinted 1997, Amber-Allen Publishing. ISBN 1-878424-26-2. Roberts, Jane (1977). The World View of Paul Cézanne: A Psychic Interpretation. ISBN 0-13-968859-5. Roberts, Jane (1978). The Afterdeath Journal of An American Philosopher: The World View of William James. Prentice-Hall. ISBN 0-13-018515-9.

"My religion is kindness. A good mind, a good heart, warm feelings, these are the most important things."

The Dalai Lama.

www.ingramcontent.com/pod-product-compliance
Lightning Source LLC
Chambersburg PA
CBHW060053100426
42742CB00014B/2814